GHOST STALKER II

*A psychic medium visits
Europe's most haunted castles*

D0097270

GHOST STALKER II

A psychic medium visits
Europes's most haunted castles

Michelle Whitedove

WHITEDOVE PRESS

In some instances the names have been changed to protect individuals privacy

WHITEDOVE PRESS
C/O Book World
1941 Whitfield Loop Rd.
Sarasota, FL 34243

www.MichelleWhitedove .com

To order additional Copies of this book 1-800-444-2524

Book Design by ColorCraft 954-345-1002

Photography by Maliena Slaymaker

Printed on Acid Free/Recycled paper
Printed in the USA

Library of Congress Control Number: 2004106989

ISBN# 0-9714908-5-6

First Edition

10 9 8 7 6 5 4 3 2 1

Lost Souls

Tortured souls on a dim lit night,
Unknowingly create an ethereal fright.

We turn to them at shadows hour,
Asking them why they haunt this tower.

Ere the night grows long and cold,
The dust filled rooms are far too old.

Walking toward the cellars keep,
Wondering if these ghosts will stop to weep.

Do they fear what we don't know,
Or do they wish to be left alone?

I seek these specters of ancient lore,
Asking them please to open the door.

Their angels seek them, as do I,
Wishing them to please, not wail or cry.

Heaven is but a reach away, waiting to shed light,
Much like the day.

So blow away the cobweb dreams,
Forget the petty murdering things.

Take Gods hand and fly away,
So not to haunt another day.

- Maliena Slaymaker

Dedication and Thanks

My gratitude as always is for the support and protection that I receive in abundance from my guardian angels and spirit guides. I am thankful to God first and foremost for the council and clarity in all my travels. Without this direction of my support team this book would not be possible.

It is very important that I acknowledge Maliena Slaymaker and give her due credit. As my photographer, researcher, and friend, I can honestly say to my readers that this book would not have been completed without her efforts. She was my rock and support at a very difficult time in my personal life, during the process of writing this book. Thank you Maliena for all of your hard work and helping me see this project through.

To my best friend and partner Shante, I thank you for standing by my side and supporting me. She sees in me what I sometimes struggle to see in myself. Thanks for your love and devotion to all of our projects over the years.

Special thanks to Michael Woodard for his hard work and time that he gave to this book in the editing process, especially with regards to the limited amount of time given to you.

Special thanks to Gary Marshall who has been an integral part of all of my books. These published works would not be of the superb quality that they are without his help. His creative efforts in book design have been inspiring for me as well as others. Thank you Gary for your important role. You are a truly wonderful soul.

CONTENTS

TALKING WITH SPIRITS

rom first hand experience I can tell you that stalking ghosts with Michelle Whitedove is always an adventure. While touring America with her, we stayed at Myrtle's Plantation situated deep in the bayous of Louisiana. This 1790's bed and breakfast is rightfully touted as "America's most haunted home". On the last night of our stay we were up late doing a ghost vigil. At three in the morning Michelle spotted a ghost on the front lawn, She told one of the girls to film the area with her night vision camera. With the naked eye, none of us non-psychic ghost enthusiasts could see the specter. But when the video was replayed, sure enough I witnessed my first ghost. A bright orb of light, which looked to be the size of a tennis ball, was bouncing in mid-air across the front lawn. After about three or four bounces, the light transformed into a glowing man walking with his arms swinging. He took a few steps, then returned to the form of the shining orb. We were all transfixed, watching the video over and over again.

The very thought of ghosts challenges us to rethink our perception of reality. And each of us must decide for ourselves. Are hauntings merely a figment of an overactive imagination or are there invisible souls wandering this earth? For me, my personal reality was changed forever when I saw the ghost captured on film.

The unknown has fascinated, yet frightened us since the beginning of time. And Michelle Whitedove's mission is to educate humanity on spiritual topics as well as the paranormal. Who better to educate us than a person with supernatural powers; someone who can see into the future and also look back in time. Information gleaned not from so-called history books, which are colored by the writer's political and personal views, but from a **clairvoyant's** vantage point. Whitedove can look at history through truthful eyes, receiving **psychic** visions of real events, without bias. As a **spirit-medium**, she is gifted with the ability to converse with the unseen souls that inhabit the space right next to where you are sitting at this very moment. Her **channeling** abilities enable her to receive information directly from the source - whether it is a ghost, an angel, an entity, or the universal consciousness that opens for her like an endless encyclopedia of mystical knowledge.

Michelle is not limited to speaking to the dead but, in this book, it is her focus. I have heard Michelle lecture on many topics throughout the years. But some people wonder why anyone would want to research earth bound souls. "You cannot deny the fact that darkness exists here on earth," said Michelle Whitedove. An upbeat spiritual education, guardian angels, spirit guides, the soul's evolution, and positive thinking, are what most new age people prefer to deal with. But Michelle refuses to only educate us on the feel good topics. She wants us all to realize that the journey of the soul is multifaceted and there are many paths that a soul can follow.

Throughout our trek to Europe's haunted and sacred sites, I was constantly amazed with Michelle's insights. Using her highly developed psychic abilities, she would receive information about a ghost or a location, and shortly thereafter receive confirmation of her psychic accuracy.

This book was not written for the faint of heart. It is a glimpse of another reality, one that is not pretty, and one that is not fantasy. Ghost Stalker II is overflowing with information that is usually privy only to the few unique souls that have the ability to walk between worlds. So, get ready to experience the unknown as Michelle Whitedove unravels some dark mysteries.

With best intentions,
Shante Powders

PS. For actual photographs of this trip, go to
www.MichelleWhitedove.com

"Reality is merely an illusion, albeit a very persistent one."

-Albert Einstein

MYTHS, LEGENDS
AND LORE

The trip to England started out much like my ghost trip across the United States, only I had planned to pursue much older ghosts; specters of ancient castles, coaching stops known as pubic houses or pubs, and hotels that are centuries old. The United Kingdom gave us an ancient history adventure that America could not compare to in age.

As you will see, the UK held much more in store for me than ordinary ghosts. This book contains some exquisite ghost encounters but also a lot of bone-chilling European lore that I feel should be discussed, even if only for a brief chapter.

Of course, it's only appropriate to start this chapter by discussing ghosts, so let's look back at Europe's ghostly history. I would like to talk about how long ghosts have been documented and what people thought of them hundreds of years ago.

Ghosts have been documented in all parts of the world, but nowhere as much as in Europe. Hundreds of years ago, Europe was filled with extremely superstitious people; crazy folklore was strongly believed in, and it was thought that ghosts were evil and would torment you until the end of your days. Some people even believed that to see a ghost could result in your death or, at the least, bring you a string of bad luck. In ancient times, people warded spirits off with talismans, herbs, and rituals. There were even ridiculous phrases that people would use to ward off ghosts, like this one from the 1500's; *"If you see a ghost, walk around it six times, and it will disappear."* Of course, today most of us think it's amazing that people ever bought into such nonsense. As a spirit-medium, I can tell you that ghosts are only as good, or evil, as they were in life. Seeing a wayward spirit will not bring a curse upon you, and I assure you that walking around one six times will only make you dizzy! Keep in mind that ghosts are as bewildered by our presence as we are by them.

Ghosts are human souls who are unable to move into the light for a variety of reasons. As a result, they are stuck in limbo somewhere between our world and the next, tracing reality only with their wispy forms and frightening echoes. To my knowledge there is no recorded date of the first ghost sighting. I believe that this is due to the fact that life and death on earth are synonymous. Since the first humans began to experience death, there have been those who became scared or confused at the time of their dying and were unable to travel into the light; the result is an earthbound spirit. But, having said that, also remember that ghosts have choices in death just as they did in life. No one is doomed to roam the earth as a spirit unless they choose to. Unfortunately, with all the misconceptions about death, some souls do stay behind instead of traveling to the light. In time, though, whether it's a year or three hundred years, these ghosts will find their way back to the heavens.

Some people will go through their entire life without ever coming into contact with a ghost, but the rest of us will have a tale of witnessing an orb of light, a streak in our vision, or even an actual transparent human-like manifestation. If you do ever happen to see a ghost, there are a few things to keep in mind. If there is a ghost in your home, or if someone close to you has passed away and you believe they are earth bound, then light a white candle, and pray for them. Your positive prayers will help guide them to the protective white light of God. In most cases you do not need to be afraid as few ghosts will become violent toward humans. Even if they are malevolent; most of them are incapable of creating the tremendous amount of energy it takes to physically harm us. In my experience a wayward spirit usually will only be able to pinch, or lightly push. Last but not least, be compassionate. All ghosts were once living, breathing beings who deserve compassion and respect from those they encounter. No matter how lost or ethereal they seem, they are still God's children just as you and I.

Wayward spirits are not the only supernatural phenomenon in which people believe. There are endless tales of creatures said not to exist, yet, in the back of our minds, we all wonder..."what if?" The rest of this chapter is a short dedication to three such creatures; an afterthought if you will. A chance to open your mind to unprecedented knowledge of supernatural beings.

Ghosts, though not believed in by all, are pretty much universally accepted. It's hard to ignore their presence and even non-believers can't totally disregard the numerous stories that they have surely heard throughout their lives. After all, so many well-documented accounts could not all be faked...right? But what about other European creatures that lurk behind the outskirts of our reality? Let us take a look at some other myths. I've been directed to set the record straight on three such beings of lore - the werewolf, the vampire, and the witch.

A Witch is a person who is said to possess magical powers, with the ability and knowledge to cast spells and use other magic. However, like most mysteries in the world, witches cannot be defined through the use of a common dictionary. So, let's look back at a moment in time that is commonly referred to as, "The Witch Craze".

The persecution of supposed witches lasted from the late 1400's to the mid 1700's. That is almost three centuries of unjustified fear and cruelty inflicted on humanity. Over one hundred thousand people were put on trial, most of whom were found guilty and subjected to torture before being hung, drowned, or burned at the stake because they were accused of being witches.

In this day and age, history tells us that most of those indicted as witches were simply healers and midwives using the tools that nature provided to aid them. In general, they practiced healing with the aid of herbs and perhaps they would **scry** for the future on occasion. So, the real question about witches is why were they feared and thought to be so evil?

The witch hunts have been blamed heavily on the church's influence over the people, and while, yes, the church persecuted witches, it stemmed more so from secular governments which decided whether or not witches would be hunted in their lands. Since it was widely believed that a witch could infringe on a king in the worst ways possible, causing turmoil for his country, many kings were in favor of seeking witchcraft out and destroying it. This led to a frenzy of paranoia and accusation, not just from kings and magistrates, but also from the local townspeople's suspicions which seemed to know no bounds.

As an example of the gross embellishments that people came up with, here is a quote from Martin Luther in 1522. *"Sorcerers or witches are the Devil's whores who steal milk, raise storms, ride on goats or broomsticks, lame or maim people, torture babies in their cradles, and change things into different shapes so that a human being seems to be a cow or an ox".* Now that is a rather unbelievable description for someone to live up to and even though there may have been a witch or two with some such powers, there were not more than a very few.

Are there authentic witches? Was there any validity to these historic hunts? Using my abilities to channel information, I asked for clarity and information on the topic of witches. In reality, most of these supposed witches were nothing more than earth mothers - women who worked with natural herbs and doing what they could to help heal those in need. Many of them subsequently suffered the horrendous punishment of torture and death as a result of their good deeds.

There are two different types of witches. The first is what is referred to as a "Natural Witch", meaning someone who is born a witch - a person who doesn't have to learn spells, but who naturally possesses magic.

Truly, this is the innate power of the person's will and invoking their word. These individuals have a powerful mind and are often able to think of something, then have it occur without any physical activity; what I refer to as instant manifestation. Most of these natural witches have healing abilities and some can even foretell the future. Sometimes, there are even physical signs you can look for that are called the mark of a natural witch; for instance, being born with a **caul membrane** covering a newborn's face, webbed toes, or albino pigmentation. Red hair can also be the sign of a natural witch (of course, not all red heads are witches). Being born with six fingers or toes is also a magical sign. Interestingly enough, Marilyn Monroe was reported to have six toes and Freud was born with a caul - lucky for them to be born in modern times.

The other way to become a witch is through the practice of "Wicca". Although the word Wicca is a fairly modern Anglo Saxon word that stems from the root word, "to bend or change", the belief itself is one of the oldest religions in the world. You do not have to be Wiccan to be a witch, but they do often go hand in hand. Natural witches are far less common than practicing Wiccans, but both are legitimate.

At times, it worries me, to see a teenager intently reading a book of spells he or she picked up. For the spiritually uneducated, dabbling in spells can be a dangerous business; there is powerful **karma** at work for the practitioner. For those on the good path of helping others, and for those into the dark arts for personal gain, the effects of their manipulations will be returned to them ten fold. It bewilders me why anyone would want to hurt another with such severe karmic repercussions.

The main lesson that mankind was supposed to learn from the witch craze is that we humans have an innate lack of tolerance, especially concerning things we do not understand. We always seek to kill what we fear.

The green-faced witches with warty noses, riding on broomsticks and terrorizing villagers, are a farce. Our group consciousness has to recognize that we put thousands upon thousands of people to death out of our own ridiculous fear. This is a lesson that we must learn so we don't keep repeating the same mistake when the next unexplained phenomenon occurs.

The second, most well documented European myth, if you will, is the werewolf. There are several theories behind the idea of humans turning into wolf like creatures. In 1591, a German man named Peter Stubbe, was the first human to be tried and convicted of being a werewolf. The villagers had been chasing a wolf-like creature through the forest, and upon finally cornering it, they set their dogs upon the beast. But, instead of running away, it stood up on its hind legs and changed into a man - that man was said to be Peter Stubbe. He was arrested and later confessed to over sixteen murders with detailed accounts of how he would turn into a werewolf and devour human flesh. Peter was sentenced to death and the world had just recorded one of the first Werewolves, but certainly not the last.

The more popular belief among the scientific community is that humans do not take on a physical change, but a mental one. A term was even given to this "disorder" - Lycanthropy. Lycanthropy centers on the idea that the cerebral tissue in the brain begins to deteriorate resulting in psychological damage which causes the patient to exhibit strange animalistic behaviors. One woman began to complain of a strong urge to eat raw meat, and succumbing to overly aggressive sexual behaviors. During a full moon, her husband even caught her in the kitchen howling and walking around on all fours, naked. She was eventually placed under psychiatric care and with the use of antipsychotic drugs they were able to control her wolf like behaviors.

But if Lycanthropy is the explanation to all Werewolves, then why have so many people claimed to see large furry beasts roaming through the forest, tearing people apart? How did the legend become more about men changing into a half wolf creature by the light of a full moon? Some say it's a type of devil worship, and that a potion was rubbed into the skin to cause this transformation. Others say it's a curse placed on men that forces them to turn more and more into a wolf by the waxing of the moon. Thousands of people in Europe during the middle ages were accused of being werewolves and when found guilty, they too were burned alive.

In the most famous case of all times, a Werewolf by the name of "La Bete" began terrorizing the French village of Le Gevaudan from 1764-1767. Few people that lived to speak of it saw this Werewolf, but in every eyewitness account the description was the same. A large beast that stood on two legs, reddish fur with a black stripe down its back, a bushy tail, and two small horns resembling that of the devil protruding from it's forehead.

This Werewolf killed over one hundred people and finally the village was so terrified they sent word to King Louis XV who sent soldiers out to track down and kill the creature. They eventually found La Bete and shot it repeatedly until it fell. Still, the soldiers did not want to get too close, so believing it was dead, they left the werewolf's body in the forest. Within two months, the killings began again. All of this is well acknowledged through signed documents in which a witness was required to be present. You can still see original wanted posters that were made in an attempt to rid the village of the werewolf.

Later, the king's best wolf catcher was sent to the village. After inspecting La Bete's latest victim, he came to the conclusion that no ordinary wolf could be responsible for killing the villagers. The paw marks the wolf catcher had discovered around the victim were so large that he believed the beast may have been the size of a cow, with the ability to leap a distance over twenty-four feet. After three years of torment, the villagers took matters into their own hands. They tracked La Bete and managed to kill it...this time they burned the werewolf's carcass and the attacks completely ceased.

But many of the facts about the "La Bete" Werewolf remain inconsistent with our modern day myths. For one, La Bete hunted almost exclusively during the day. Secondly, silver did not kill it, but rather several wooden spears. I discovered through extensive research that silver was actually a Hollywood concept with no real validity. The idea behind the silver bullet was simply created to add more drama to the film. Most recorded historical cases involving the killing of a werewolf state that normal weapons worked just fine. The events of La Bete have become so infamous that Hollywood successfully distributed a foreign film called "Brotherhood of the Wolf" which was loosely based on this true story of the French Werewolf. Whether or not La Bete was a human turning into a werewolf, or a strange wolf-like monster that was never human, still remains a mystery. When I asked my spirit guides for some clarity regarding La Bete I was told that it was never a human turned wolf, but it was in fact a werewolf of sorts; a creature from another realm. At one time werewolves did roam earth and if they bit a human that human would turn into a similar creature. However it's time on earth has come and gone. There are no more creatures like La Bete here, at least not to my knowledge.

The last myth that I would like to touch on is the ever so popular and romanticized vampire. This is perhaps the most difficult of the three legends to discuss, partly because, in this day and age, the term "vampire" is so loosely used. Vampires do exist, although most people find the notion ludicrous. Not to say that there is a devilishly dark and handsome man slumbering high in a castle tower tempting virgins to their eternal fate...but not to say there isn't either.

Most popular of course is the "human" vampire, a person very much alive who chooses to live a vampiric lifestyle; feeding off of another person's energy, drinking blood as a ritual and emulating the things a vampire would do. But let's face it. Those vampires, although interesting, are not the immortal seductresses that we would normally think of.

Sometimes, human vampirism can be taken too far. The oldest and best example would be Elizabeth Bathory. Elizabeth was born in 1560 in Transylvania and was considered to be the most bloodthirsty woman ever to live. She came from a royal family and had many powerful relatives. She was married to Count Nasdasdy when she was just fifteen years old. From the beginning, it is said that Elizabeth was an evil woman who would torture and maim peasant girls. Her husband was called the "Black Hero of Hungary" and his deeds in war amassed him even greater wealth. This gave Elizabeth even more freedom to conduct dark and evil experiments on servants and unlucky travelers who would not be missed. Her husband would also partake in these tortures, even teaching her techniques he learned in war. He bought her various torture weapons including an **Iron maiden**. Among her demented tendencies, Elizabeth was fond of drinking the blood of her victims.

Elizabeth left her husband for a short time. Of course, this was unheard in those days. The villagers reported seeing her with a dark, sinister-looking man they said had sharp teeth and pale skin. Knowing that she was evil, they whispered rumors that she, in fact, was a vampire. But, within weeks, Elizabeth returned to her husband and he forgave her indiscretion. Then, in 1604, her husband died of multiple stab wounds of unknown origin.

The years passed and Elizabeth continued to torture and murder people by the hundreds. As she grew older, she became fearful of aging because she was considered one of the most beautiful women in all of Europe but her extreme vanity caused her to desperately seek a way to stay young. She thought that, by bathing in a virgin's blood, she had discovered eternal youth. In 1611, Elizabeth's murder spree was unraveled and she was arrested for the murder of six hundred and fifty people. The high number of victims only added to the villager's suspicions that she was part of a coven of vampires. All of her trusted servants who had aided in the murders were executed, but the government punished her with solitary confinement rather than death. Since the town owed Elizabeth a large amount of money, it is thought she was allowed to live in order to not have to repay the debt.

Elizabeth's family managed to keep her from attending a trial and instead she was walled into a single room of the castle where she remained until her death four years later. Gallows were erected on each corner of her castle to warn people that a creature of horrible nature dwelled there. When I channeled information about this story, I learned a great deal. I was told that Elizabeth was responsible for her husband's death as she murdered him when she tired of his company. I also asked my spirit guides if the stories were true. Was Elizabeth in fact a vampire like so many of the villagers had thought? I was assured that she was not. Elizabeth was aware of them, though, and many of her blood offerings were made to the immortal creatures she so longed to become.

However, most Vampires are said to be "Undead" and, therefore, no longer human at all. In fact, many of the older stories speak of creatures that sleep in graves and come out only at night to feed. When these vampires are found they stink of death and, if they have recently fed, their bodies are bloated with fresh blood. During this trip, we traveled from Scotland down into northern England, and took the time to stop in a small town called Melrose, most famous for its beautiful abbey. Melrose Abbey has a vampire story of its very own and it's not only well known, but respected because the abbey's very own monks documented the events that transpired.

According to the transcripts during the twelfth century, a monk who was said to be lazy and callow, lived in the abbey. He was nicknamed the "Hound Priest" for his love of hunting dogs.

The Hound Priest unexpectedly died and was buried in the abbey's cemetery. Shortly after his death, a woman came to the other monks in the abbey asking for help. She claimed the dead monk was visiting her from his grave at night as she had seen him tapping on her window and it was horrifying her.

Naturally, the other monks were more than a little skeptical, but they agreed to watch for him. Taking shifts, they stayed near the Hound priest's grave with an axe in hand. Upon the very first night of keeping watch, the monk on guard rushed in to wake the others claiming that, in fact, the dead priest had attempted to rise from the earth. The monk said he had struck him with the axe and the Hound priest then returned to his grave.

The next morning they exhumed the body and discovered a large axe wound in the hound priest's side as well as fresh blood along the bottom of the coffin, proving that he was in fact a vampire. With no other choice, the monks burned the body of the hound priest and spread his ashes into the wind.

These are just two of many documented stories about vampires; valid stories that simply are unexplainable. So, as you go through life undaunted by the far-fetched tales of creatures most don't believe in, remember that all legends are born of some sort of truth!

Throughout our travels in the United Kingdom, we experienced a multitude of supernatural occurrences, and like my first Ghost Stalker book, I felt it was important to document everything that we experienced exactly as it happened. So, please venture with me into the realm of European ghosts, specters, and ancient mystical sites. I included the brief history of each location, a detailed travelogue of our exploration and, of course, my channeled information at the end of each chapter. Thank you for stepping into this journey with me. I hope you enjoy it.

In Love and Light,

Michelle Whitedove

"Fear is the main source of superstition, and one of the main sources of cruelty. To conquer fear is the beginning of wisdom."

- Bertrand Russell

DALHOUSIE CASTLE
BONNYRIGG, EDINBURGH, SCOTLAND

HISTORY

The Castle Dalhousie was built in the thirteenth century although most of what you see today is dated around 1450. The Ramsay clan held possession of the castle longer than any other family in Scotland. The castle sits next to the South Esk River by thirty-seven acres of forest and garden, and even has a chapel nearby where ancestral relics still rest. Like all things, change has come with time and eventually this castle was sold and converted into a twenty-seven room upscale hotel which remains a popular site for romantic weddings.

Dalhousie comes from the ancient French word "Dalwolsie", which means, "meander in the river." When the castle was originally constructed, it had a drawbridge and a dry moat. The drawbridge was the only way to enter the castle, and through the centuries, bits of the castle were added as well as destroyed. In fact through the castles modern day entrance you can still see the mechanisms that lowered and raised the drawbridge.

The Ramsay name was first heard sometime in 1140 and is said to be the first family to have owned land at Dalwolsie. The first Ramsay arrived in Scotland after following King David the First. From there, the Ramsay name continued to appear in history and they even became famous during the border raids. William Ramsay was a strong English supporter at first. According to legend, King Edward I slept at Dalhousie Castle the night before he finally defeated William Wallace. Despite this, William Ramsay eventually joined forces with Robert the Bruce in 1314, to help appeal to Rome for help against the English.

In the following centuries, the Ramsays of Dalhousie proved their loyalty and strength to Scotland. Great stories are still told about the various lords of Dalhousie castle, but maybe none as great as Sir Alexander de Ramsay. In the mid 1300's, Sir Alexander and his knights had begun to raid the English borders. After he freed the last Scottish castle of Roxburghe, King David II was so grateful that he made Sir Alexander Sheriff of Teviotdale, as well as Roxburgh's constable.

Unfortunately, one of Alexander's rivals was so infuriated with jealousy that he kidnapped Alexander and let him die in the dungeon of Hermitage Castle. Sometime in the late 1800's, his remains were found and returned to Dalhousie.

Not only did Dalhousie castle represent a noble family line of Scotland, but also the unrelenting resistance to English tyranny. In the 1400's, King Henry IV of England attacked the castle. The siege lasted over six months but was unsuccessful; Dalhousie castle stood fast.

The Ramsays continued to grow in prestige and, by the 1600's, the family had been granted Earldom. By the 1700's, Dalhousie had been home to five Earls and the family was now more involved with politics than bloodshed.

The ninth Earl of Dalhousie died in the late 1800's and his son became the only Marquis of the family. When he died there was no living heir, so a distant cousin came to possess Dalhousie effectively ending the Ramsay's occupation of the castle.

Today, Dalhousie Castle is considered a luxury country hotel, featuring twenty-seven bedrooms in period furnishings, complete with two restaurants offering traditional Scottish cuisine, the Aqueous Spa, and an aviary. It is also home to a much-photographed ghost.

JOURNAL

Scotland, March 11-12

I arrived in Scotland at three o'clock, accompanied by Shante my best friend, and Maliena, my photographer. After an uncomfortable sixteen-hour flight and dead on our feet, (no pun intended) we jumped on a shuttle to pick up our small four-door rental car at the airport. For an American, getting into a car with the steering wheel located on the right side is unnerving, but starting the car and driving on the wrong side of the road is just plain traumatic. To add to my personal panic our maps were insufficient. Major highways were noted, but many roads were just nameless lines on the paper. The addresses we did not understand; I swear they looked more like a license plate number. There are no street numbers, nor street names, so how were we supposed to find our first destination, Dalhousie Castle, Bonnyrigg, Edinburgh, Scotland EH193JB?

Driving in Scotland was only our first dilemma as foreign tourists. Thank goodness, Dalhousie was only fifteen miles from the Edinburgh airport. Everyone we met was helpful in giving directions, but even good directions proved confusing. As an American let me just say this... "forget our four way intersections where you stop and wait your turn!" Most of Europe does not believe in actually stopping; they have roundabouts instead. These are circular intersections, much like a wheel with spokes. You enter a roundabout by merging with the traffic, going clockwise, until you reach the correct "spoke" or exit. There can be as many as five exits per roundabout and you better hope that you know where to exit, or you'll be on that thing forever, just going around and around in a never ending, never stopping, circular nightmare! As I'm sure you've guessed, our merging techniques needed a bit of perfecting; we were being honked at regularly as a clear reminder. No, we didn't turn out to be Scotland's best drivers.

We arrived in the countryside just before dusk. Entering a long driveway, the castle seemed to be hidden from us as we drove down a deep ravine, rounded a corner and went under a tall ancient bridge made of two gigantic stone arches. The panoramic view was absolutely beautiful. A rose colored castle stood in the distance, perched on rolling hills of the greenest grass, surrounded by forest and a light fog in the air that added to the majestic scene. Approaching the front of the castle, we noticed the massive oak door that was once part of the drawbridge and a dangerous two-story drop off the side of the building that is the remnant of the dry moat which once helped to protect the castle.

The red stone towers encased the interior gray walls of this pristine castle from the 1300's, one of Scotland's finest.

We walked inside, noticing right away the unique and beautiful ceiling of the two-story foyer. The white walls vaulted up high to meet a turquoise arched ceiling ornately outlined in bronze colored plasterwork. Still further up in the center, was a windowed **cupola** that allowed light to stream down through the quarterdeck. Closer to eye level, the plaster detail was very curious. The white cornice trim was decorated with a row of different men's faces. They were carved around the perimeter of the room, and each of their noses was covered with a white sash, as if to say, "You stink!"

The seven flights of wood stairs creaked upward to Suite Twenty-Four at the very top of the castle's tower. We followed the porter as he told us that our room was the most haunted. We neared the top and the stairs began to narrow. As we tried to catch our breath, the porter dropped our bags inside the door and quickly made his exit. The cool stone walls breathed an ambiance of ancient Scottish heritage. At the very back of our medieval suite was a small staircase that led up to a platform and, standing on my tiptoes, I could see out of the window set high in the room. We could hear birds chirping and their clawed feet clicking as they walked back and forth on the roof. The wind continued to howl through our room and, gazing out over the moat to the forest line, I began to think about how this was the same view that the castle inhabitants had seen centuries before me.

After retiring for the night, we spent the next ten hours sleeping off jet lag but woke up that next morning ready to go. Breakfast was the first thing on our agenda. We headed down the stairs to The Orangery, which is a conservatory or what we might call a sunroom. This glass-encased restaurant gave us an expansive view of the forest and river below. Wanting to immerse ourselves in the local culture, we decided on the traditional Scottish breakfast which consisted of eggs, haggis, blood sausage, and, much to our surprise, baked beans, small whole mushrooms, and grilled tomato. Shante and Maliena both liked the haggis until later in the trip when they found out that it is made of sheep's stomach, heart, and liver mixed with some oats and seasoning; not exactly the kind of breakfast that we are used to. I found the blood sausage so scary I couldn't bring myself to taste it. As I looked about the room, I observed that none of the locals ordered the Scottish breakfast and you can bet that I didn't order it the following day either.

The Orangery is also the site of a fairly recent ghost story, not the ghost of a human, but the ghost of an animal. A number of people have claimed to see the black shadow of a dog outside, staring in through the windows at night. The trouble is, there are no dogs anywhere near the castle, no tracks have ever been found, and no barking or howling is ever heard, so what could it be?

In the mid 1980's, a dog lived at the castle by the name of Petra. Apparently, Petra somehow fell out of one of the towers plummeting over a hundred feet to its tragic death. At night, the ghost of Petra is said to pace around the outside of the castle, pressing its nose against the windows and frightening guests. But the hotel staff assures their guests that Petra is harmless. Still, those who see the ghostly dog can't help but find it disturbing.

Next on the morning's schedule, we embarked on a falconry tour that is offered on the castle grounds. We walked down the dry moat along the river's edge with the falconer and his Harris Hawk. Each of us was given a thick leather glove, and, once far away from the other birds, the young man holding the tethered hawk would set the bird free whereupon it would soar across the river and perch high in the trees. We took turns bringing the bird back to our gloved hands which were baited with raw chicken meat. The falconer told us about "The Sport of Kings" and the interesting facts about each of the birds in the aviary including a Red Tailed hawk, an Eagle, a Falcon, a Kestrel, and a variety of different owls. Among them were an Arctic Owl named Navajo, that was almost two feet tall, and a tiny owl named MacBeth that fit in the palm of my hand.

As we walked around, the castle hovered above us in the distance, a light mist grabbed at our ankles, and we pulled our coats up closer as the chill of the wind whisked by. I asked the young man about the ghosts of Dalhousie and he grew somewhat solemn. He told me that he himself did not believe in ghosts, but that he also did not enter the castle. He worked only outdoors, but he did mention that his employer had several experiences in the castle while working, seeing furniture moving by itself, feeling cold spots and hearing heavy footsteps when no one was there. The clouds in the sky seemed to darken briefly as he rushed through the story. Ill at ease, he told us we'd have to speak with his boss if we wanted any further information. I let it go at that and we finished our tour.

The hawk walk lasted about an hour and a half; being so in tune with nature was a wonderful experience. After the falconry, it was off to Edinburgh, so we hustled back up the seven flights of stairs to gather maps, coats, and wallets, then back down to the car.

Originally, we had planned to visit the famous "haunted" Edinburgh castle, but we were sidetracked and never made it that far. We parked at the Royal Mile, which is the oldest part of the city and opted to walk around to the different shops. The weather was biting cold and damp. We decided to stop at a pub for fish and chips. Maliena tried to get used to their strong warm beer. As for me, my soda came complete with one ice cube. After warming up, we spent a few hours milling through the cobblestone streets and open plazas. We had decided to try our luck with a haunted tour called the "Underground Tour" which was supposed to lead us down into the old vaults that lie beneath the city of Edinburgh. At around seven o'clock, we found ourselves outside of Saint Giles' Cathedral at the Mercat cross for the tour.

Most villages and cities in Great Britain have a "town cross" which is a large carved stone marker that looks like a miniature tower. Each town cross is built at the heart of the town's center. In days of old, this was the place where the people would gather to have public meetings and official proclamations would be delivered. The Mercat Cross was the site where Bonnie Prince Charles was pronounced king in 1745.

Town markets were also held here, goods were sold or traded and justice was doled out in the form of hangings, floggings, and other methods of public humiliation and punishment. The parliament building was to the rear of Mercat Cross, which is why there were full executions here as well. Although a bloody and violent courtyard, I did not feel any spirits wandering around at this place of much death.

We gathered in the town square to be a part of the Mercat Underground Tour, which was supposed to be a historically accurate tour of the underbelly of the city. We were three of a tour group of twenty, watching skeptically as our guide began squawking out stories of the most barbaric kind. He was an actor, and we were his unfortunate audience. We were being dragged along the streets of Edinburgh and I really don't have words for this tour other then the familiar phrase, "Remember the Alamo." Only, in our, case it was "Remember the Queen Mary ghost tour!" The outrageous display of over-acted Scottish lore was accompanied by ridiculous audience participation such as mock whippings at the Mercat Cross, which, to me, felt condescending, considering that men and women really were tortured for centuries at this very place. As far as the scary part is concerned, we heard several ghost stories most of which held little truth and the occasional high-pitched outburst from the guide to try to unnerve the crowd.

The second place we walked to on the tour was a place called "Mary King's Close." The morbid history behind this street is so horrendous and upsetting that I hate even to write about it. Giving you the edited version of this historic story is more than graphic enough.

During the middle ages when Edinburgh flourished with people as well as their filth, the plague attacked this city with a vengeance, so much so that thousands and thousands of villagers became deathly ill. The people of the city were terrified and did not know how to stop the plague or even how to slow its growing body count. Fearing that the black plague would soon kill all of the town's people, a gruesome decision was made. They decided to take all of the sick and place them into one district called "Mary King's Close." This area is made up of several closes that are considered narrow alleys today. After every last ill person had been relocated to this area, the Burg Council had Mary King's Close walled up. Without food, water, or medicine the plague victims would die an exceptionally painful and cruel death.

For weeks, the people of Edinburgh were haunted by the cries for help from within the plague stricken street, until the very last soul in Mary King's Close had perished. Weeks later, the town had to find a solution to the foul smell that the hot, June days had left for them; thousands of bodies were now rotting in the close. Baking in the summer sun, there was an unbearable stench, even for these people who lived without sewers. It was finally decided that a group of Edinburgh workers would go back into Mary King's close and dismember the bodies of the plague victims in order to dispose of them as quickly as possible.

In the early 1900's a series of apartments were opened in Mary King's Close, but they were short lived. Any one who attempted to stay there was driven out by the ghosts and other supernatural activity that continued to occur. Even after a hundred years, tenants were still reporting specters; and it didn't take long for this close to gain the reputation of being evil, vile, and not fit to live in. To this day, people still claim to hear disembodied voices begging for help and other such ghostly experiences.

Eventually our long-winded guide led us down the ancient side streets of Edinburgh's Royal Mile into the deep belly of the city. We walked down a steep staircase and he opened a large padlocked wooden door was the entrance to the vaults. This was by far the most authentic part of the tour even though it was hard to get a look around with all the dramatics and crowded groups of people. These vaults looked like a series of wine cellars, with compact dirt floors and barrel shaped ceilings of brick and stone. Some rooms were two stories high and nearly thirty feet long. Others were only eight feet high and ten feet long.

We walked from room to room, maybe for a half-mile when, thank God, our first ghostly visit occurred. A young woman to the right of us happened to take a picture in a vault about halfway through. She used a digital camera and after hearing one particular frightening ghost encounter she looked back through her snap shots. The last picture she took revealed a rather large orb in the center of her photo. Bright white in color and round in shape, it was most definitely a spirit... a Ghost!

The spot where the picture was snapped has an odd story in itself. It is said that a female ghost is trapped in the corner of this room: she is malevolent and when people get too close, she will attack them! This ghost has been known to leave deep scratches on her victims, but our guide told us she is unable to wander because another ghost in the same room prevents her. I stood there not paying too much attention to the gawking tourists who were all craning to see the girl's picture. The room we were in is called the "cobbler's" vault because the ghost of a shoemaker is said to linger here. He is also the ghost who supposedly keeps the evil at bay. Suddenly, I began to feel some unseen force tugging at my left foot. Gently at first, then gradually a little bit harder until I could no longer ignore the spirit responsible. He definitely wanted to let me know that he was there. This spirit didn't mean any harm but it is always precarious to feel a ghost next to you. I moved up a little, and the spirit followed me, still tugging at my foot. Our guide went on to tell us about another ghost that prefers this room, all while I was overcome by the presence of the cobbler. We finally left the room and the tugging stopped as soon as I walked out. Let me quickly add that, in regards to the female ghost in the corner, I could not feel a strong presence. If she is there, I can guarantee it's not because the cobbler keeps her there. Souls are never limited to one space. They may choose their preferred residence, but I assure you they are not confined as souls travel at the speed of thought.

Regardless of the lack of supernatural activity, these vaults contained many imprints. I could feel the energy of another time period. Feeling the emotions of thousands of souls is powerful in itself. Psychically, I could see how the city worked centuries ago. The energy, even now, is still connected to that time and I could feel how sick the people were who worked and lived in the vaults. They had no fresh air down there and no clean place to live. This created pestilence, lung sickness and death to many of the residents in the vaults. It was also home to a seedy side of the law; brothels flourished there and syphilis was rampant. Body snatchers hid out with their decomposing loot as well as pickpockets, robbers and maybe even a vampire or two. These people were like moles, living their lives underground and rarely seeing the light of day.

The vaults are a very vast area, concealed below most of the city with tunnels and small iron gates sealing off passageways to other parts of the underground city. Our tour guide perhaps told us only one sincerely frightening thing on our way down. He said, "don't wander off because the vaults are enormous, winding in all directions... and if you become lost, it could take a very long time to find you again!"

Most of the tour group was not privileged to see what I did. All that they saw was some very authentic looking black cobwebs and our guide, in a black cape, swirling around the dust-filled rooms. Don't get me wrong, just the idea of seeing below the streets of such an infamous city was well worth the six pounds, but don't be disillusioned into thinking you will see some supernatural occurrence simply by reputation.

When we finished the Mercat tour, we called it a night and headed back to Dalhousie castle. We were still getting use to driving in Scotland. There were so many roundabouts that we made a wrong turn in the dead of night and, in doing so, returned to the castle much later than expected. When we entered, it was obvious that a wedding had taken place. There were women in gowns on the arms of men in kilts roaming throughout the castle. Shante, Maliena and I decided to head down to the library for what we hoped would be some quiet time to catch up on our notes. This castle library is very cozy, with a coal-burning fireplace, in an intimate setting filled with couches and high-backed leather chairs; perfect for quiet conversations. We found ourselves sitting on a comfortable sofa next to the large, lead-glass window that overlooked the river. The walls are covered with honey-colored bookcases full of interesting old books. I took special notice of the magnificent ceiling with large, white plaster seashell motifs in each corner just above the cornice with white plaster scrollwork that highlighted the bold, terra cotta colored ceiling. This was a wonderful atmosphere in which to write, however, half a glass of wine later, we found ourselves surrounded by the groom's parents and various other family members who abruptly ended our quiet time. They were a friendly and funny group of Englishmen who had made the long trek from London up to Edinburgh to see their middle son married. Although they were English, the groom's father wore a kilt to show respect to his new daughter-in-law's family heritage. It was rather amusing to watch the older man sit on the couch awkwardly, paying no mind to the position of his legs as his wife chided him, saying that it was improper to sit that way in a skirt. "Not to mention," she said scandalously, "Scottish men don't wear underpants beneath their kilts!" It was hard to stifle a laugh, and soon we were tempted into casual conversation. We discovered the skeptical English minds of our new friends. The men were total nonbelievers, even going so far as to say that ghosts and haunts are things only women and children indulge in. I tried not to be too offended as I noticed that, despite what they said, none of them would dare stay overnight at the castle.

By midnight, the evening was winding down and the wedding guests were heading home. Shante and Maliena decided to have one last drink before turning in, thankfully! As fate would have it, a very generous employee of the hotel, by the name of Peter, arrived at the library to take any last minute drink orders.

Shante hastily stood up and placed the order; little did she know that wasn't all she would get. He engaged her in conversation and soon it was discovered that he could give us a "proper" tour of the castle and show us what was hiding between the walls of what was now a grand luxury hotel. Pointing to a bookcase, Peter showed us that in this very room, there was a secret passage that was discovered in the 1700's. Today, you can see the doorknob on the faux bookshelf that leads you into a hidden, but fully functioning, service bar. When the door is closed, though, the entrance is obscure and easily blends in with the collection of leather bound books that surround the wall and the open fireplace. Although today it is just a hidden room with only one way into the space, intuitively, I knew that this was once a secret passageway used for escape down into the secure areas in the lower part of the castle.

Ecstatically the three of us jumped up and prepared for a history adventure. The first place Peter took us was into a large sitting room called the Dalwolsie room. This second floor room overlooks the front of the castle and was originally the place where the lord conducted his business matters. It was here that Peter showed us the floor that gradually sloped in an upward angle so that no guest would stand above the lord. Sure enough, though I am only five foot five and Shante is an easy five foot ten inches tall, when I walked to the end of the room she and I were suddenly eye level. Legend of the castle tells us that the great William Wallace was six foot six inches tall, so this optical illusion flooring came in handy to match the lord's ego with his perceived height. On the wall of this same room, there hung a picture of Catherine, daughter of one the Ramsey's **lairds** from around 1720; so scorned by his daughter's promiscuous behavior that he locked her in the highest room of the castle, which of course was the tower suite where we were sleeping. The young girl vowed to get revenge and eventually she starved herself to death, although it is said that she died of a broken heart, and now her spirit is condemned to walk the castle halls. The picture of Catherine is so haunting that it's hard to accurately describe. She sits alone on a puff stool with her hands in her lap in a very lady-like manner. Her disposition is very fitting; her mouth shows only a slight pouty smallness to it. Yet, somehow, there is an underlying sadness in her that can't be explained; some sort of knowing, making it seem like she was destined to become a ghost.

From there, Peter led us out of the room into the main hall and down past the grand staircase where he revealed a mysterious discovery. First, he showed us two false walls and two staircases that lead you in separate directions. One dropped off into nothing, which at one time used to be another dining room. The second one started in a closet but then, after the fourth step, was met by a stone wall.

Next, Peter walked us halfway down the hall and stopped at a door that was only about four feet high. He opened it slowly and revealed to us a stone spiral staircase that led downward. He said with a very thick Scottish accent "Now girls, go down if you want to see the "real" dungeon."

Once through the small wooden door, we could stand upright. The narrow stairs lead down sharply perhaps twenty steps or so. As we reached the bottom, there was a wall of glass that separated our stairs from what looked liked an underground wine cellar. Peter told us that, in fact, yes it is a wine cellar now, but once was a thirty-five foot drop into a dank dungeon in which the castle held its captives. The only way to access this dungeon was to use a rope and lower prisoners their food. At the end of their confinement, if there was an end, that same rope would drag them back out. Today, you can still see the deep groove in the stone where the ropes left their marks. Peter mentioned that usually when a prisoner was sent to the dungeon, they were simply pushed off the ledge and left to fall down the long thirty-five foot drop into the blackness. I'm sure that the fall alone broke many bones and killed more than a few men. There was a dark, sad energy to the room that could be felt even through the pane of glass that now separated the stairwell from the drop off into the dungeon.

When we had originally arrived at Dalhousie, the staff had encouraged the guests to eat their meals in the restaurant deep down in what they said was the dungeon. In fact, the fine dining restaurant's name is "The Dungeon." However, now we had discovered that, over the centuries, this castle had been dramatically changed and we were just now getting the real story. At that point, our tour was interrupted when Peter's beeper went off and he was summoned back to the library to pour cocktails.

After Peter's departure, Maliena and I ran upstairs to retrieve camera equipment and a voice recorder. We jogged back up the never-ending staircases that had become our nemesis. I was in such a hurry that I didn't bother to shut off the TV that had been left on and remembered only to lock the door.

We caught Shante still waiting for Peter to return and we ended up in another amusing conversation, this time with the bridegroom who was dressed in a kilt and vest. He was gloriously drunk and quite happy to make our acquaintance. In a good-natured tone, he scoffed at the idea of ghosts and casually enticed us to crash his post wedding celebration in the library. Finally, his beautiful bride dressed in a red silk Indian Sari found him and coaxed him to return with her to join their friends and family.

Peter discovered us in the open foyer called the quarterdeck, and we were elated to continue on with our private tour. He told us that this area is used for many wedding photos. People love to sit on the large, throne-like chair in the center of the space, and, in fact, a photographer had recently captured a ghost on film. We walked down one flight of stairs to the registration area that was underneath the quarterdeck. Behind the hotel's front desk, Peter pulled out a binder and turned to a photo of an elderly gentleman, dressed in evening attire, sitting in the regal chair as his elegant wife stood beside him. In the foreground of the picture, standing between the photographer and the couple, was a distinct outline of a human form, but it was made of ethereal mist. Yes, it was an authentic photograph of a ghost who was enjoying the wedding celebration. The spirit was just milling around with the guests and quite taken with the festivities.

He said it is not uncommon for guests to complain of a tingling, cold feeling that passes through them, especially during weddings. Dalhousie has had more than just one ghost sighting. There are also rumors of a butler seen in the restaurant area. The odd description of this ghost is the fact that he appears dressed in a suit and covered in cobwebs. Another woman is also said to haunt Dalhousie, but nothing is really known about her.

Peter showed us how the castle was mostly built in two separate time eras and that the original castle was sort of in the middle; the newer additions were built out and around it. He also told us the story of a little page boy that used to work in the castle. He was gentle and dim-witted, but he held favor with the lord of the castle. Despite this, he once was locked into a room as punishment and was accidentally forgotten. For whatever reason, the child was not discovered until centuries later and the ghost of this boy is still said to be there.

We ended the tour in the Dungeon Restaurant. The gray stone floor and enormous walls vault up to a fourteen-foot, arched cathedral ceiling. Tables were set for a gourmet meal with candles, and white linens covered in crystal goblets. In the dim lighting, you could see two sixteenth century knights in full metal armor standing guard in the arched recesses of the walls. Their shadows made them tower over us. Their shields and swords close by, they seemingly watched our every move and it felt very creepy. Although this room looked like an actual dungeon, Peter told us that, ironically, it was still holding the same purpose it always had. This stone-fortified room was once the "Castle Keep" - a secure area where the lords had stored food, ate meals, hung slaughtered animals for feasts and stowed weapons and other valuables that needed to be kept safe during a raid. After seven hundred years, this room is still intact and serving its original purpose, only in grand style.

The night was soon over and we thanked Peter for his hospitality as we headed once again to the top of the castle. Our suite was, as I said, the same fateful chamber where Lady Catherine had met her self-inflicted death. As soon as we entered, psychically, I could feel that something was amiss. The energy seemed more charged than it had felt earlier. Nothing looked right, and the TV, which Maliena and I both knew had been left on, was mysteriously turned off! The wind rattled the thin-paned windows and the chilled air was unsettling. We walked around the room looking for signs of an intruder, but, of course, there were none. I made a bad joke that perhaps Catherine's ghost prefers books rather than television. No one laughed. Maliena stood up and told us that she was going to take a bath to relax. Seconds after the door closed she burst back out with a frightened look on her face, telling us to come quick. She said when she had entered the bathroom, she was met by an unexpected surprise. Shante's plastic bottle of liquid soap had been crushed almost in half. A crescent gash was torn from the side of the bottle and it looked as if someone had purposefully flung it around the tub area. A large swirl pattern of yellow liquid soap was squirted on the bottom and sides of the tub, as well as up onto the walls. Yet, the bottle itself had been neatly placed back where it originally sat, near the faucet. Maliena was understandably upset by this ghost's violent crime scene. The three of us sat down on one of the beds to regroup. The temperature in the room seemed to drop even more and the howling outside was not helping the situation. "Why would a ghost be so intent on breaking things?" asked Maliena. I reassured her that it was just mischief and to not worry so much. After we got our wits back, I was able to show Maliena the bright side. "Hopefully Catherine liked the honey scented soap, because in her day, baths were a rare treat!"

CHANNELED INFORMATION

The Vaults - Edinburgh Underground

My guides started the channeling session by telling me that the cobbler who tugged on my foot is an active ghost in the vaults, but that most of the ghostly activity here is actually just energy **imprints**. The people who are capturing photos with globules and orbs are usually capturing an actual spirit. But there are also energy imprints that are left behind. An imprint, if you don't remember from my first book, is a scar on time projecting through our dimension; a lot like a movie scene of a historical event, usually a tragic one, playing over and over until the energy eventually fades away.

The woman in our group, who had caught a spirit on film, had indeed captured the ghost said to reside in the corner of the cobblers vault. This is a ghost from the middle ages. In life, this woman ran a shop in the cobbler's vault and, when she died, she created a reality for herself. She believes that that she is still working in the vault and that this place is still filled with the people of her time. This ghost is not trapped in that corner; she stays there because in life it was where she worked - her station, if you will. If she feels stuck, it's by her own limitations as she is not held there by force. My guides showed her to me with some detail, she worked with her hands, wore a dingy apron and was as bitter and miserable in life as she is now in death. The cobbler and her knew each other, as they worked closely together, and they both died at the same time of the plague.

The vaults also contain a vast amount of energy from past vampires. At one time, they lived in these vaults. The vaults were their lairs; they were able to feed on the people who lived down there in the darkness. There, they could be concealed and humans would often protect them. At one time, it was a safe place to sleep away from enemies and to stay hidden from the sun. By the time that hundreds of people started to live down in the vaults, the vampires had already moved on. The plague also offered these creatures an ample supply of bodies to feed on as the diseases did not affect them.

Dalhousie Castle

There are some faded energy imprints, but Catherine is the strongest ghost at Dalhousie. In fact, I feel that she is the only one left, although at one time this castle housed five. People have claimed to see different ghosts in different areas, but it's usually her they are seeing. She is the one who always walks around, who is captured in the photos, and who is so often felt during the wedding receptions. Catherine doesn't usually manifest in the shape of a woman, but rather as mist or as an **orb** of light. She is still quite attached to the tower room where she died and is not fond of the humans that invade her castle home. Although not a violent ghost, she does small things to put off guests and staff alike.

The story of the butler covered in cobwebs did not bring any information forth. I would say that he is a ghost story that is entirely fiction.

The dog Petra was not a ghost either; at least not in the way, you might think. Petra is an animal spirit that was connected to one of the men in the castle. However, when he left, so did the dog's spirit, although I do detect the faded energy of Petra which is most likely what people have seen. Many times when beloved pets die, their spirit hangs around their owner. Their loyalty continues even after death.

The little pageboy is also nothing more than fading residue of castle life. He was a ghost here for a short time but, luckily, he was able to cross over into the light. Eventually all souls return to heaven. It is where we all come from, and the place where we reside between incarnations. In life, this boy was an orphan who held favor with the lord of the castle.

He would run about the grounds, do errands and odd jobs, disappear for a while and then show back up; no one paid him too much attention. He was not punished, as legend says, but rather he accidentally locked himself into an area where he should not have been. There are many secret passages and secure hiding places at Dalhousie. Unable to get himself out, he eventually died. The lord did look for him but, as this was during a time of war, they assumed the boy had run off or had been killed. That is why his body was not discovered until years later in a sealed off portion of the Castle.

"Do I believe in ghosts?
No, but I am afraid of them."

- Marquise du Deffand

DALSTON HALL
CARLISLE, CUMBRIA, ENGLAND

HISTORY

The city of Carlisle is in the Northernmost part of England, however, some may say that the city should be part of Scotland. For centuries, Carlisle was a border town but, regardless of that territorial dispute, the first recorded community was Roman, established around 120 AD. There is still a Roman wall near Dalston, along with many other Roman influences.

After the Romans left, the Danes invaded sometime in the fifth century. By 945, the Scots had become the enemy and destroyed most of Carlisle, leaving the city in ruin.

For many years, Dalston Hall was inhabited by Scottish rule because, at this point, the Scots had the upper hand. As the border wars continued, and the land of Cumberland changed back and forth, the manor house of Dalston Hall eventually came to rest with the

Earl of Cumberland in the 1300's. Thus was established the wealthy Dalston family, who transformed the Hall into the fortress that then protected the English family from the frequent Scottish raids. Over time, the hall was built onto and became not just one mighty tower, but two. On the second tower there is mysterious writing carved into the side. It is written in old Gothic script and, when translated, it reads something like "mi wifs tower." The really interesting part of it is that, not only was it written in a script no longer used, but it was written backwards. By 1157, the city of Carlisle was again in English possession where it has remained ever since.

JOURNAL

March 13th - 14th

We woke up Saturday morning ready to say goodbye to the southern parts of Scotland so we could make our way into the northern tip of England. From Dalhousie castle to Dalston Hall was just under a two-hour drive through the deep, thick, green valleys of Scotland via the scenic route. There was a slight mist in the air and the two-lane road wound through pastures filled with sheep and stone walls. Midway through the drive, we made a stop in the small village of Melrose on the Scottish border. There we visited a large medieval ruin called the "Melrose Abbey" which had been home to an order of Cistercian monks from 1146 - 1544. It's rose-hued stone spires towered at least a hundred feet into the air overlooking an ancient graveyard with decrepit head stones, dragons and gargoyles as well as other delicate carvings. Michael Scott, a thirteenth century wizard, is said to be buried in this abbey, along with his book of magic.

The town itself seems to honeycomb up around the abbey. From a distance, the abbey looks like a large, functioning cathedral but, as you get closer, the monastic buildings are shown to be crumbling. Despite this, it's majestic nature seemed unyielding. This is a very holy place. In 1329, Robert the Bruce, one of Scotland's greatest heros, requested that the abbey should be protected for all times. He also requested that, upon his death, his heart was to be buried there. When he eventually did die, his body was buried in Dunfermline, but a knight on crusade fulfilled Robert's wish and brought his heart to the abbey where it was buried under the chapter house for safekeeping.

We spent a couple of hours wandering through the massive abbey, climbing up to its very top, for a bird's eye view of the surrounding countryside, and later walking through the ancient graveyard. Old gravestones are always fascinating to me. There was one depicting a man carved of stone lying atop his final resting place. I have to admit, it was shocking to see how small he was. Centuries ago, most men were small; about the size of a twelve-year old boy by today's standards. I noticed that many head stones bore a skull and crossbones on them and it occurred to me that this had a significant meaning. I wondered if it was some sort of religious sign or an indication of death by plague. Unfortunately, no one could answer that question for me. We took many photographs, purchased some postcards and Shante bought a bottle of **mead**. As we left the Abbey grounds, we stopped at an antique shop to browse and ask for directions to Carlisle. There, we spied the most darling confectioners shop I'd ever seen. We purchased several pastries and a Scottish Tipsy cake, which you must try if you ever find one.

We arrived in the bustling town of Carlisle around six o'clock but, by the time we made it down Dalston road, it was closer to dusk. Dalston Hall was gorgeous; a beautiful fortress with two stone towers and big, heavy oak doors leading into the dark paneled foyer.

We checked into rooms four and five. My room was large and beautiful, definitely made for a woman.

The bathroom was egg shaped with a low ceiling and a footed tub in the middle.

As I waited for the girls, I ran my fingers across the mantle and I felt a very strange and tingly energy on the right side of the fireplace. Later, Maliena stood in the same spot and mentioned a similar feeling, which was when I first became aware of a female presence in the room.

Still waiting on Shante, we fumbled with the television set to turn it on, and then headed down to meet up with Tony Walker who operates a company in the United Kingdom called "White Rabbit Leisure Tours". He was very helpful in making suggestions and ideas while we were putting our itinerary together. In fact, he had pointed out to Maliena that the order in which the trip was scheduled, was not north to south like she thought, but rather a zigzagged mess. Much planning goes into a road trip on a different continent and it just happened to work out that Tony was going to be at Dalston Hall the same time of our stay. He has done many ghost hunts throughout the United Kingdom and is very knowledgeable on the hall's haunted history.

We joined him for a wonderful meal of sea bass and venison in a quiet dining room lit with silver candelabras. It was relaxing after our drive from

Scotland. We then decided to tag along on Tony's private ghost tour that he was giving to another couple. He told us stories about each room in the fortress and we were able to visit every room except the owner's apartments. His history of Dalston Hall was very interesting and it was really good to have it on record; many of the stories he told us matched up with the ones we had been able to uncover through our months of research.

Several ghosts are said to roam the grounds of Dalston. In room four, where I stayed, there is a ghost said to reside near the bay window. She was named "Sad Emily." Her apparition gazes out onto the front lawn below and, because of her despair, the room, although beautiful, has a deep, melancholy energy attached to it. Psychically, I had already felt a ghostly female presence and this story was just confirmation, but something told me that Sad Emily wasn't through with us yet!

Another woman called "Lady Jane" oldest ghost the most well-documented. She is seen dressed in a Tudor-style gown and is sometimes spotted walking up and down the front hall. Tony also told us about "Mr. Fingernails," a dark creature seen by very few, who lurks in the cellar and sometimes floats up through the floors of the great hall. The entity supposedly is malevolent in nature but does not appear to venture too far from it's primary haunts (pun intended).

Throughout the cellar, loud bumps and footsteps can be heard but, perhaps the most noticeable of such, is the sound people have reported of wooden barrels being rolled. This is supposed to be the ghost of a workman who spent most of his life laboring and he truly loved it. The sound of the rolling barrels is attributed to the beer kegs that the worker would move around.

The entire fortress is a maze of hidden tunnels, sealed off stairwells, and various rooms. I picked up on the fact that most of Dalston's secrets have yet to be uncovered. As we continued on our tour, we walked up the spiral steps to the tower at the very top. Through one door, we were able to walk across the roof via a small platform and make our way to the tower on the opposite side. The night was cold and windy and the moon offered little in the way of light. The miniature flashlights we carried were our only real protection. Small drops of rain had begun to make the walkway slippery and dangerous as squalling winds whipped my shawl around. Struggling to keep our balance, we all made it safely to the other side.

Entering the tower door, we continued up more spiral stairs, until we finally beheld the wedding chamber. This room was unique; the walls were made of cut gray stone and the floors were built-in levels with a four-poster bed on the top platform, giving it a very regal look as it sat pressed against the rear wall. Yet, I couldn't shake off an uneasy feeling. In fact, the room did not exude love and wedding bliss, but felt icy and chaotic, instead. Tony told us that this room was originally the room that served as protection from invading enemies. Many members of the Dalston family had been forced to hide in these quarters. They were isolated from the world, listening hour after hour to the sounds of screaming and pounding, as the invaders tried to break down their iron doors to kill them. Luckily, none of these attacks were ever successful as the fortress always held fast. In fact, the centuries-old, hand-forged Iron Gate at the bottom of the steps, is still in place. Despite the perilous history of the room, not many ghost stories have been reported in this area. Most reports involve couples feeling a bit uneasy and not wanting to be left alone in the room, along with a few tales of men seeing a ghostly woman, dressed in white, floating across the bathroom. The wedding chamber may not be as haunted as the rest of Dalston hall, but it still has a supernatural charge to it that's hard to ignore.

From there, we ventured back down to the second floor. Room twelve is supposed to be haunted by two girls who are benevolent and full of laughter, but it is not the sense that you feel. This room is perhaps the best room at Dalston, mostly due to its huge bay windows that overlook the garden and its access to the second story terrace. Room twelve also has a potentially large bathroom to add to its attractiveness, I say potentially because, at some point, the bathroom was split in half. There is a portion of the bathroom that is sealed off with no way to get in or out. No one knows why or when it happened but, if you step outside, you can peer through a small window and see the unfinished, partly plastered room with wood and debris scattered about. It looks like who ever did seal this room up, did so quickly and quietly.

The other problem with room twelve is that the energy takes on a very malevolent form, despite the sweet, giggling girls. There is no documentation to shed light on the reason why this room is so haunted, but most people believe the secret lies within the sealed off portion of the bathroom. Many people have woken up while staying in this room and asked to be moved because they felt uncomfortable and frightened.

The giggling girls have also been heard in a few of the other rooms in this section of Dalston. There have also been numerous isolated accounts of supernatural visions. Guests have claimed to see small children running about; the ghost of a man in room eight has been reported several times. We were told that one psychic who was walking down the west hall toward room four, said she clearly saw a man in a leather jerkin walking by. The disturbing part of her vision was the fact that he was dragging a young girl by the hair who was screaming and kicking. When he reached the end of the hall, the man preceded to fling the girl out of the two-story window after which he disappeared. The way this story was described to me, I would be more likely to think this man was not a ghost, but an **imprint**. It makes sense because he is committing a horrible act, so the energy is most likely repeating the scene over and over until it fades away. It is a visual scar on time and space, not an actual spirit or ghost who possesses the ability to move and make decisions.

Although one sighting alone is not strong enough to confirm this imprint's validity, as we were being told this tale Maliena snapped a picture of the area. When our film was returned, it showed not one, but two ghost faces on the back of Shante's pant leg, as well as several orbs in the upper left hand corner.

The clearest of the two ghost faces is of a man's side profile. He is angry and aggressive, and his features are strong and very definable. Could it be that we had stumbled across not only an imprint, but also the ghost who, in life, had created that imprint? I'd never come across anything like it before and time would reveal the outcome of this new investigation.

The last ghost to be documented at Dalston Hall is that of a caretaker. He is from the Victorian era and can still be seen today, walking the grounds. There isn't much information about him, other than the fact that he committed suicide by hanging himself from a tree not far away. Legend says the tree promptly died and all the branches were cut off, but the tall trunk still remains. We took a picture of this tree and it is, indeed, ominous and sad. You can even make out what looks like a face in the trunk area, which, in itself, is scary.

Eventually, we ended up in the bar for coffee and soon I excused myself for the evening. Picking up on the impressions of the history, and all the souls who have made the grand mansion their home, had exhausted me and I needed some alone time to really tune into the barrage of psychic information.

Back in room number four, I saw for myself that there really was a ghost who resides here. While lying in bed, I was suddenly disturbed by a movement out of the corner of my eye toward the big bay window. When I glanced over, I realized that the metal window latch was being pushed up and over by an invisible hand. A chill ran down my spine and I looked away hoping it would stop. However, the ghost continued to lift and push at the latch until finally I had to get up and open the window. This seemed to make the ghost content and the movement stopped. Soon after though, I saw my ghostly roommate who was sitting in a chair to the left side of the fireplace. This spirit, who had been falsely named "Sad Emily," again was trying to get my attention. The spirit communicated to me telepathically that her name was really Katherine, spelled with a K. She said that she was waiting for her lover. She made it clear that room four was her room and she wondered why people kept invading her private space. She mostly sits by the fireplace but, at times, she will pace to and from the bay window gazing out waiting for her lost love. As I was connecting with Katherine, Maliena and Shante were with Tony, trying to soak in more history.

That night we got a feeling for Dalston Hall and visited with Tony and the owners who were wonderful to us during our stay. At one point, Maliena had closed her eyes to meditate and a girl came to her - not physically, but mentally. She wore a blue party dress, with a choker around her neck, and she looked very young. Her brownish-hair was tied back in a bun and she had light green eyes and a hint of freckles across her nose. She seemed to be from maybe the early 1800's. She spoke to Maliena and showed her a cameo that she loved. She also informed Maliena that a picture of her had hung in Dalston Hall for many years, but it had recently been moved which was upsetting her. As quickly as Maliena had seen this vision, it faded. The experience seemed so real that she told Shante and Tony about it. He said it was uncanny because, only weeks earlier, the new owners had taken most of the old pictures off the walls and replaced them while moving several others around. Everyone was stunned and began to look around in an effort to locate the missing picture. After an hour of searching around, even finding stacks of pictures piled up in the cellar, they agreed it was way too daunting of a task to complete. Suddenly, the owner's youngest daughter came up to Maliena and Shante and handed them a medium-sized, framed painting of a young girl. She looked very much like the one Maliena had seen during her meditation and it was dated 1800. The picture had been removed from the hall and obscurely placed in one of the downstairs bathrooms. Whether

Maliena experienced a surge of intuitive information or an actual spirit was never fully revealed, but one thing is sure; we had not entered that bathroom, nor did we previously know about the pictures being moved around.

After midnight, the girls came to my room for an impromptu tea party. Hotel rooms in the United Kingdom are all supplied with an electric teapot, along with a selection of teas, cream, and sugars. We snacked on some little teacakes that we had purchased in Melrose, and shared information. Finally, around three in the morning, we called it a night, unsure of what would happen the following day.

The morning came quickly, and by nine-thirty, we went down to breakfast. We inquired about the traditional English breakfast and, laughing, we requested that they hold the beans. It's so odd that baked beans, the American camping food of choice, is their fine breakfast food. Our table faced windows that looked out to the gardens. It was a blustery day and a red squirrel was happy to entertain us as he scampered around the patio in search of his own breakfast. The morning was chilled and quiet so we decided to go back to our rooms for more rest. Quite comfortable in the plush beds, the three of us slept well into the afternoon. Around 2 pm I began to feel restless, so after making some entries into my journal, I went for a walk on my own.

The grounds around Dalston Hall are also very haunted. Tall, brown, withered trees jutted up into the gray sky, shaking in the wind. Their muddy, yellow leaves on the ground whisked around me in various whirlwind patterns and leaving me with a deep sense of isolation. Maliena had taken this same walk earlier in the day and snapped some photographs that I hoped would turn out as ominous as the area felt. On my way back to the hall, I found the tree which legend says died immediately after a gardener hung himself from it. All the branches were cut off and, today, the massive stocky trunk sits alone, dead, and sad. I also saw that face in the bark, staring at me as if to warn trespassers of the death and sorrow it has been subjected to.

I walked back along the edge of the forest and made my way behind Dalston Hall, where I spotted the writing on the second tower which was written backwards. Roughly translated, it means, "this is me wife's tower" although it's impossible to read if you don't know what it says beforehand. Why it was written on the tower, let alone backwards, is still a mystery to this day and one I meant to try and unravel.

It was around five o'clock when the three of us met up again for dinner. The dining hall was empty and peaceful as we ate yet another wonderful meal. The owners made cheerful conversations with us that eventually led to more talk of ghosts and the history of Dalston Hall. Since the previous owner's daughter had tragically died at Dalston, the grief-stricken parents had refused to go back. Even reluctant to show prospective buyers around. The new owners, Jan and his wife Karen, fell in love with the beauty of Dalston Hall, but, they too, soon wondered about the supernatural activity in their new home. Already, in less than a year, they have lost the business of a regular guest or two because of ghosts. In their most recent experience, a business man who had frequented Dalston Hall for years, had been preparing for bed when he saw the door handle begin to move on it's own. The next morning, he came downstairs, shaking, and informed the owners that he would not be returning.

Around ten in the evening, Maliena and I went up to my room to grab our flashlights. When we entered the room, she flopped down on my bed facing the window, chatting to me casually, as I pulled my hair back into a bun at the vanity. As I listened to her, I was suddenly struck with a surge of cold that went right through my chest and out through my back.

I staggered backwards from the force of it, shuddering violently. Maliena had stopped talking and her eyes were wide open. "Michelle, did you see that?" she asked, but I was still trying to catch my breath. "The entire bed shook beneath me, it felt like an earthquake," Maliena said. I told her what I felt and she jumped off the bed a little wide eyed. Maybe we startled a ghost or it was irritated by our presence. Whatever the cause, we were both ready to get out of room four! Katherine's ghost will tolerate men, but has a habit of making female guests feel unwelcome in her room, I had even heard stories of women waking up to growling noises from under the bed. It would appear that this ghost goes to great lengths to rid herself of living company and, tonight, she had once again succeeded.

Making our way back down to the wood-paneled bar, we joined the others. Gathered around the coal-stoked fireplace, we sat in leather-backed chairs and listened to each other's tales while indulging in warm brandies. The lights began to flicker on and off in a teasing fashion. The owner's dog, that had been brought in for a short visit, was pacing uneasily. Karen said no matter what they did, the large German Shepard would never settle down in the bar. The dog, Frey, was sensing the supernatural forces lurking around.

As the lights continued to go off and on, Karen told us that the only time the lights flicker is if she is running some specific equipment. She made a point to tell us that, at this time of night, electricity usage was at its lowest and that there is no reason that the lights in the bar should be flickering. There were a few uneasy laughs, and Sam, her youngest daughter, was now very intrigued and a little spooked.

Outside, we witnessed another phenomenon occurring. Through the large window, we could see the hotel entrance spotlights periodically turn on. The motion detectors were being set off, and that was triggering the spotlights to intermittently light the area. They should only turn on if someone is passing by, but I never saw a man or animal in the vicinity... at least not of flesh.

As we got ready to start walking the grounds, Maliena ran back to room five for her camera but, when she got to the door, she realized she had forgotten the key; she also saw that the door was actually cracked open. Now, what is strange about this, is that the heavy doors close on a spring hinge. Only hours before dinner, Shante had commented to me on how hard the doors always slam shut behind us (they also automatically lock when the door shuts). But, this time, the deadbolt on her door was still locked, so the only way Maliena could have been able to push open the door without the key, is if a supernatural force was at work - something holding the door ajar or just playing with her. Not wanting to explore the possibility alone, she grabbed her gear and hurried back downstairs, the door slamming shut behind her.

Perhaps one of the most interesting things that came up was during a discussion we had in the bar. The owners and I were discussing ancient times of Dalston Hall because I had already received a lot of psychic information about the ghost of Katherine. I said that this ghost had told me she was waiting for her lover to return from far away and that he was off fighting in a war. Katherine had lived sometime in the late 1700's; she was deeply in love with this man and just realized that she was pregnant. Her lover never returned to her, so she remained at Dalston Hall even after death, which I felt may have been caused simply by a broken heart. She seemed to have withered down to nothing until she eventually died.

I also felt that the man Katherine waited for had traveled away by sea. I asked if the ocean was close by and I received a great confirmation. The owner's eldest daughter told me that, indeed, Carlisle used to be a major port to the Irish Sea and that there was still a fishing channel fairly close to Dalston Hall. None of us Americans had any idea the Irish Sea was so close - we thought it could be anywhere from two to four hours away. Confirmations like this are important and let me know that I am on the right track. My psychic information was accurate and well detailed.

One of the great things about Dalston Hall is the fact that they still have many of the original record books from as far back as the 1600's. The present owners thought it was amazing that I had gotten information about the port, but they had no verbal history about this Katherine of the late 1700's, or who she may have been. So, Shante spent several hours reading through these huge logbooks, most of which contained property deeds, death and birth announcements and various financial accounts of the family business. There, in this old, tattered book, full of dust and grime, was detailed information (as I had earlier said), about a woman from the same time era, who had lived and died at Dalston Hall. The written facts fit my psychic information too closely to be mere coincidence. This was great to have in writing, as I obviously could not have known this before hand.

Another detail that came up was the fact that, despite all of the old ancient cemeteries in Carlisle, and despite the fact that the Dalstons where a wealthy prominent family in the community, not one single gravestone had ever been found! How, in times of old, when families could not and did not travel far, could there have been no graves for a religious, God-fearing family such as the Dalstons? I was finally able to receive some psychic visions that provided the answer.

First, I was shown that Dalston Hall has been drastically changed over the years as entire sections of the great fortress are hidden and walled off. I got the strong psychic impression that many rooms and tunnels were hidden below the cellar of Dalston. In fact, the owners are contemplating whether or not to knock out a wall in the cellar because they need more storage space. In the back room of the cellar you can see through some small fist sized holes. You can peer in and see it was once a room. It appears to go back at least thirty feet and, before it was walled off, someone or something filled it up with rubble and trash. There is simply no way to tell what is beneath the mess, but it must be the size of a fairly large hall. I said that among, other things, there is a hidden tunnel that will lead them to a church in town. The owners later confirmed that there had been a rumor of that tunnel, but most people thought it would be impossible to dig almost a full mile. I assured them it was not impossible and it is still there, intact, waiting to be rediscovered. Karen then showed us another walled-off passage that she was aware of. In the main baronial hall, beside the dining room, is a cloak closet. When you open it, you see a staircase that has been blocked off by a wall after only a few steps. Only when you bang on the wall do you realize that it is hollow.

Another possible reason for all the supernatural activity at Dalston Hall is something that I picked up on during this channeling session as well. I told the owner that, below what is now the library, but was once the Dalston chapel, is either an open mausoleum or a catacomb. That is where the ancient bodies of the Dalston Family still lay and the sole reason that graves had never been discovered of the Dalstons in the local graveyards.

Maliena is educated in European history and confirmed for us that it was common practice for wealthy families to bury their dead below their private chapels, especially during times of war, so that they could prevent the graves from being robbed and defiled. She said, in fact, that the word "Pew", as in the church benches, gained its name from the stench that the bodies gave off when they were left below the chapel.

I recommended to Karen and Jan that, should

they choose to try and dig up the entrance, they leave the bodies to rest in peace. They agreed. Jan then went on to say that, just outside of the library he had recently discovered, that a large, flat stone in the floor was loose. Upon further inspection, he realized it could be pulled up, revealing some sort of opening that was now filled with loose stone and gravel. He had not even told Karen about this yet, but he wondered if it was an entryway to somewhere.

After a couple of hours, I was desperate for a bottle of water. Karen offered to go into the cellar to fetch one and Maliena agreed to accompany her since everyone was a little spooked. While down in the cool basement, Maliena noticed a small wooden door in the beer keg room that had a crude wood latch to keep it closed. When she asked Karen where it leads, she said she had never looked. Of course, curiosity overcame them, and they couldn't resist taking a peek. But at the exact moment when they opened the door, right behind them a soda line exploded and made a loud, high-pitched shrieking sound that caused both Karen and Maliena to let out a blood-curdling scream. Nerves now sufficiently shot, they quickly looked through the small door. They observed a covered manhole and a small tunnel to the right, though neither of them were about to creep in further to see where it led. Karen quickly grabbed the bottle of water and they ran back up the cellar stairs only to find another shock waiting for them.

At the top of the stairs stood Frey, Karen's large german police dog. They said he looked as confused and startled as they were, and Karen was flabbergasted as to how he had escaped from their apartments in the back because the door locks when you leave; of course, locked doors are never a sure bet in a haunted building. Karen quickly ushered him back to her apartments before heading to the bar where the rest of us were waiting.

Finally, it was getting late, the hotel guests were all in their rooms, and the staff was gone. It was well past midnight and the three of us, along with their daughter Sam, headed down the giant hall in search of ghosts, while everyone else went to bed. The first place we ventured to was the cellar. I was really reluctant to go back down because of the creepy feeling we had all experienced from the ghosts that dwelled there. Of course, Shante argued about it until I agreed; no one said ghost hunting is always pleasant. As we slowly walked down into the blackness of the narrow cellar, Maliena went on ahead to snap some photos, but, such is her luck, she soon ran out of film. Shante, Sam and I ventured forth exploring all the nooks and crannies while Maliena ran back up to the room for more film.

When Maliena returned to the cellar stairs everything was very quiet - almost too quiet. She called out our names, but we were at the very back end of the cellar, too far away to hear her, or for her to hear us. As she began to walk down the stairs, she thought for sure that she heard our footsteps just ahead and began to quicken her pace while calling out to us. At some point, realizing that now the footsteps were behind her, she froze. Aware that it hadn't been our footsteps, and too scared to turn and look at what was behind her, she tried to decide what to do next. She didn't relish the idea of continuing down into the maze of haunted rooms and passages that the cellar contained but, at that moment, it was still a better plan than trying to go back up the stairs where the disembodied footsteps were still echoing. It took one loud bang directly behind her head to send her running our way. Finally, she caught up with us near the last room where we teased her about scaring us. Pale-faced, she said, "I guarantee I'm more scared than the three of you put together - now, let's get the hell out of here!" We all let out an uneasy laugh and then quickly agreed. Following the corridor back to the stairs, we left the cellar behind.

Psychically, I was able to gain more information in the cellar. In the lower levels of Dalston, most of the energy I felt was from imprints. Ghosts from long ago once dwelled down in the cellar but, today, most of them have gone on to the heavens. The cellar's corridor still feels like a tunnel of supernatural activity and, even though a lot of it has faded, there are some spots that still feel quite disruptive. Which brings us back to an interesting tale. The staff and local ghost hunters have claimed to see the ghost of a creature, said not to be human, that dwells in the very last room of the cellar. It wears all black and it's forehead juts out in a crescent moon shape. Supposedly, it's most noticeable features are the gross, black fingernails that peek out from its robe and earning the apparition the nickname, "Mr. Fingernails." No one seems to know what exactly it is, but there is one theory about it being the leftover energy of three Scotsmen who were captured during a raid and left down there to die. I knew right away that it was not that; in fact, it's not human energy at all. I didn't receive all the information, but I definitely knew that Mr. Fingernails was from another realm.

As soon as we left the cellar, Sam excused herself to go to bed... she'd had enough! The three of us continued on, working our way upstairs to the doorway that led to our wing. We stopped in my room for a cup of tea and regrouped, making notes and deciding where to go next. As we headed back out into the hall and walked towards room seven, I remembered something that had happened the night before. I had retired early and tried unsuccessfully to get to my room but, somehow, I got turned around and ended up in front of room twelve. Twice more during the day, I started to walk to my room and was compelled instead toward room twelve again. This was disturbing for a multitude of reasons but, mostly, because the night we did our first walk through, I had a very bad reaction to that room. I couldn't get much psychic information on why, I just felt a male presence and it was very evil in nature.

Room Twelve has been a mystery to those who live at and visit Dalston Hall. The owners are renovating, but currently the bathroom is still cut in half (as I mentioned before, a whole section has been walled up). When you look from the outside window in, you are overcome by the eerie mystery that has remained unsolved for so long. As I sat in this room, in complete darkness, I was made aware that a murder had taken place in here. Hence, the negative energy that still envelops it, but I was too uncomfortable to try and channel more than that. Both the girls felt an urge to leave immediately and I, too, knew we had overstayed our welcome.

It was now late and we called it a night around 4 am. This ended our stay at Dalston Hall and, even though I was hoping for some more dramatic ghostly experiences, it was still enough to give me goose bumps and remind me that Dalston Hall is still an untapped well of supernatural secrets; secrets I wanted to reveal no matter how deep they were buried.

This was my favorite place on our trip. The service here is impeccable and the food is amazing. Whether ghost hunting or not, Dalston Hall gives you the ambiance of fine English hospitality to match its quiet country setting. If you ever happen to be in Carlisle, England, this is the place to stay.

CHANNELED INFORMATION

Melrose Abbey

Our first stop held a tremendous amount of legend and lore. Remember from the first chapter that this is the site of a famous and well-credited Vampire story. As I sat down to channel, I received a vast amount of information about the actual building. The biggest travesty concerning Melrose Abbey is that, every time the monks attempted to build on it, something would happen to prevent them from finishing. When the earliest monks lived at the abbey it was simple and plain in construction. Some parts were livable and close to completion plus, the abbey contained a vast, underground area where the monks lived and would store things. After several devastating attacks that destroyed the abbey, the monks realized it would never be completed.

Many people were buried at Melrose Abbey, mostly holy men, and some very rich people. It is true that the wizard, "Michael Scott," was buried at the abbey, and his grave was purposely left unmarked. He requested to have an unmarked grave to prevent desecration, since he was buried with his book of magic. Michael Scott was a real wizard, I could see him dressed in a full-length robe and he wore a long beard. But he was not as powerful as he was said to be and, over the centuries, stories of his deeds were greatly exaggerated. He did not part the mountains as legend says, although my spirit guides told me that he was able to cast spells and manipulate the energy around him. He was a healer and also possessed the ability of **telekinesis**, but his ego grew as he became caught up in his own abilities. Michael Scott was originally a monk and he later used his religion as a front for his supernatural talents. At one point in his life, he traveled a great deal, but the abbey remained his true home. Eventually he became a man of isolation, living the end of his life at the abbey, like a hermit.

My guides told me that the skull and crossbones seen on so many of the abbey's graves is a medieval custom; one meant to remind the living of their impending death, and also to mark where a body lay.

Dalston Hall

There was so much information at Dalston Hall that it was hard to know where to start. As I asked my guides questions, the puzzle began to fit together. Not only is Dalston overrun with ghosts, but also imprints. Sometimes it's hard to tell the two apart. The giggling girls that so many people have heard in room twelve are actually just imprints. Now, as a general rule, imprints are caused by some horrific event that creates a bleed through. However, the girls grew up playing and giggling in the hall and, because of all the supernatural energy that already ran through the building, their giggles can still be heard by some people.

Mr. Fingernails is not a human ghost, it is a dark entity. It's not really harmful, but this is where it resides and, luckily, it's not very concerned with human activity. This entity is a keeper of that particular area; not of the Dalston cellar, but of the ground that it's built upon. Dalston was built on an energy ley line and the land has a lot of magical elements. This creature is there to protect something in the earth. It has been there since long before the Hall was built and it will stay there even after the hall is gone.

The cellar doesn't contain actual ghosts, but there are many imprints and supernatural occurrences not attributed to a particular spirit. There is also a lot of activity from creatures of the fairy kingdom.

As we continued through the channeling session, Maliena asked me about the picture of Shante with the ghost face on her pant leg. I told her that it is the male spirit from room twelve and that he is the strongest resident ghost of Dalston. As I channeled information about this ghost, and of the imprints, Maliena asked me why the ghost of room twelve would be in the same exact spot of the imprint. She then asked me if it was possible that this ghost was responsible for the imprint as well. I had never heard of something like this and I eagerly asked my guides. They told me it was possible; not only is he an active ghost, but he is also responsible for the energy imprint seen in the west hallway. To confuse the situation even more, it is all directly tied to room twelve so let me try to recount the events as my spirit guides showed them to me.

The ghost of room twelve was an Englishman who spent much of his time traveling from his home in London. He would frequent Dalston Hall when visiting Carlisle and it appears he was a friend of the family. During one such visit, the Englishman murdered his mistress. A struggle ensued, he began to strangle her, and then he dragged her from their room and threw her from a window in the west hall. Not only did that leave room twelve with a vile and disturbing feeling, but it also created an energy imprint in the west hall. Every night, at the same time, the echo of the Englishman dragging his mistress to her death plays out. It is no longer a very strong imprint, which is why only very sensitive people see it, but it will continue over and over until the energy completely fades away.

This man killed the girl in a fit of rage. He had to answer for the murder of course, but since no one witnessed it, he was able to cover it up and make it look like an accident. Later, out of guilt and remorse, he killed himself in that same room... room twelve. After his death, there was an attempt to rid the room of his energy by blocking off a section of the room, probably the section where his body was found. Obviously, it did not work, because his ghost still haunts Dalston and the energy of room twelve remains unbearable. He wore a stovepipe hat, had dark eyes, a thin build, and was of medium height. He possessed a very dark look, and one may see his ghost as a shadow from the corner of the eye, or a dark silhouette. He is not dangerous to the living, though, just a dark nuisance.

There is also a dog in spirit that roams around the castle grounds, as well as inside. It is one reason that Frey becomes so uncomfortable.

The Gothic writing on the tower is a simple and loving tribute that one of the Dalstons had paid to his wealthy wife. It was written backwards, and in Gothic, because it was never intended for anyone's eyes but hers. After all, why would he purposefully disclose the location of his wife's private quarters?

I was unable to get any information on the Ghost of Lady Jane, and I feel she has probably moved on to heaven at this point.

There are many secrets at Dalston Hall, lords and owners have come and gone, many due to the supernatural. The rooms that have been filled with rubble and sealed off were done so as a taboo. They thought that they could keep it safe and put the spirits to rest, but these attempts at covering up walls and blocking rooms off to expel spirits, failed miserably. The way to expel wayward spirits is through a spiritual ritual that I call a "Clearing and a Blessing." I am often called into a place to rid it of unexplained activity - only a person with a pure heart and steadfast faith can successfully perform this type of work. I can usually make a spirit leave it's favorite haunt, although they have to choose to walk into the light.

Sad Emily, the ghost of room four is actually "Katherine" who lived at Dalston Hall and was a family member. I felt sorry for this ghost in particular and asked my guides for even further details regarding her circumstances. The man she was waiting for had made up a noble excuse to leave, but the truth was that he had another woman. Katherine was pregnant and had been keeping that news from him as a surprise. She told no one, and did not have the child because she died shortly after her first trimester. It was a form of suicide; a combination of neglect, fatigue and refusing to eat. I made a special effort to pray for her, that she may move on to the light but, for now, she will remain inside the walls of Dalston.

Beneath the library, there is a large room filled with tombs both above and below the ground, some of which are even sealed into the walls. There are treasures here; this is not a catacomb, but more like a large family mausoleum. Most of the Dalstons were put to rest here and I see from 20 to 30 bodies, both male and female. They even had a holy man that lived in the hall to oversee both church and burial affairs. Part of the underground chapel can still be seen, but it was decorated very plainly. More than seven generations of Dalstons are buried there. It has been since sometime in the late 1700's that this place was sealed off, not because it was full, but because the last of the Dalstons who lived here did so in order to protect their ancestors. There was also more than one entrance to the crypt, with yet another level underneath the first one which goes down two stories in depth.

My guides gave me very little information about the handyman, other than the fact that he did hang himself from the dead tree and his ghost still haunts the grounds, although he doesn't enter the hall itself. It is he who constantly sets off the motion detectors outside as he still patrols the well-manicured grounds.

*All houses in which men
have lived and died
Are haunted houses:
through the open doors
The harmless phantoms
on their errands glide
With feet that make
no sound upon the floors*

- Longfellow

CHILLINGHAM CASTLE
NORTHUMBERLAND, UNITED KINGDOM

HISTORY

*L*ike most castles, Chillingham Castle has a bloody history all its own. However, the bloodshed here seems more cruel and unforgiving than in many other places. Chillingham Castle is located in the northernmost part of England only miles from the sea. The castle's strategic position so close to the border played a vital part in the constant wars between Scotland and England and it was always under attack. This gray stone fortress is over a thousand years old but, like so many castles and manor houses in England, it has been built onto and altered drastically over the many centuries.

In the mid twelfth-century, the castle was little more than a single fortified tower. One hundred years later, it was granted a royal battlement license enabling it to strengthen and improve its garrisons, so more housing was added, as well as a wall which offered more protection. Chillingham was eventually transformed into a four-tower castle with an open courtyard in the center, and was continuously modified until it was utterly impenetrable; a gated curtain wall was even erected around the entire perimeter of the castle grounds.

The Grey family and their relations have been the principal owners of Chillingham castle for six hundred years. They were a wealthy family with noble titles who welcomed a significant amount of royalty into the castle. A huge stone staircase, with carved balustrades, was erected from the interior courtyard to the second story level of the castle, providing a grand entrance for any visiting King. Chillingham was also the only northern castle that had a **jousting court** where knights would come to compete.

The surrounding area held much appeal, including three hundred acres of forest that contain a rare breed of wild cattle. Visiting royalty would hunt these sacred white bulls, for various feasts and celebrations. Eventually, this long-horned herd was fenced in and protected. They have survived and can still be seen today.

Because Chillingham played an integral role in the border wars, it was home to a horrendous amount of torture. Thousands upon thousands of men died on the fields of Chillingham and hundreds more lost their lives inside the castle walls, many of which still lay buried beneath the old parts of the castle yet to be discovered.

Eventually the Grey family lost the castle which was handed down to the Tankerville family who remained in possession of it until 1933. After that, Chillingham was left unoccupied and it wasn't long before the neglected castle began to deteriorate.

Mary Grey, a descendant of the original Grey family, and her husband, Sir Humphries Wakefield, finally took over Chillingham castle and restored it to what it is today. No doubt, the Grey family is happy to once again occupy its ancestral home. Many of the antiques seen there today originally belonged at the castle and have been recovered by Sir Humphries. During the renovations, several hidden passages, rooms, and stairwells were rediscovered. This castle runs as deep as it does wide, and contains many untold secrets. Chillingham remains one of the finest examples of domestic castle architecture in Great Britain.

JOURNAL
March 15-17

We left Dalston Hall around noon on the fifteenth.

The day was young and we did not realize that the drive would take us a full three hours. Chillingham is a self-catering castle, so our first stop was at a food market to pick up supplies that we would need for the next two days. We drove across the country from the west to the northeast, following the A69. This road runs parallel to Haidens Wall, the Roman wall that was built to separate the southern civilized country from the heathens of the north in AD 122. This wall is over 76 miles long and 5 meters tall and is still considered one of the Roman empire's greatest engineering achievements. Today much of Haidens Wall has fallen apart, with the highest mark now only standing one meter tall, but it still remains the second longest manmade wall in the world with the Great Wall of China being first.

We continued our drive north into the Cheviot Hills until, finally, we made a gas stop. I could smell the salty air and knew we were getting close to our destination. The road took us deep into a valley and eventually we were in the smallest village I had ever seen. Wooden road signs showed a picture of a castle with "Chillingham" crudely printed on the side along with arrows pointing in the right direction.

I was beginning to think we would never get there when we finally saw a dirt road to the right, framed by heavy iron gates that stood open, which allowed us to enter the long, winding single-lane dirt road to the castle. It took us five minutes to creep up the drive. The tires of our car kicked up a haze of gravel and dust, and we were forced to roll up the windows. Secretly, I thought to myself, "How classic. Three unsuspecting travelers get lost and stumble onto a creepy castle in the middle of nowhere... what next?"

Large trees lined the mile long drive, their leafless fingers ominously bowed down toward the car, creating a canopy of branches high above us. We drove slowly and tried to take in the enormity of the grounds. After reaching the crest of a hill, we had our first look at the infamous "Chillingham Castle." I can honestly say that this looked like the same castle used in every horror film I've ever seen. Four-story towers flanked the ancient fortress and the weathered, gray stonework was impressive. It appeared that, despite the fact the castle itself is over one thousand years old, not much had changed. We pulled into the circle drive and noticed two black torches that jutted out from either side of the large, double oak doors. Black burns scarred the stone so we knew the torches were lit frequently. Unlike Dalhousie castle, which felt warm and inviting, this was an ominous castle. One that makes you seriously contemplate the idea of running the other way while you still can!

Stepping out of the car and glancing up, we couldn't believe our eyes as we spotted a flag with the family crest on it. The flag was flapping in the wind at the very top of the right tower. It wasn't the usual prideful lion or colorful shield one expects to see on a crest. Instead, we saw the insignia of a large black bat! Our mouths dropped open.

By the time we walked up the front steps and knocked on the door, it was dusk out, and no one answered. We pushed on the door and it slowly creaked open. I called out, "Is anyone home?" We tentatively stepped into an arched hallway as the doors shut behind us. Looking forward, we could see iron gates that separated the hallway from the stone courtyard. A wooden bench to the right let off the rank odor of a cow skull that had been left there to dry. Bits of hair and skin continued to attract flies and it made my stomach turn. On the right side of the hall was the office door. Pushing it open, we were met by Hazel, a tall, dark- haired girl with circles under her eyes who looked in need of some rest. The office was just a shabby room with a couple of desks, piles of paper and metal file cabinets. We stood there waiting as she dug around for the keys, not even pretending to give us a welcome.

Hazel apologized for her disheveled appearance, explaining that a British television crew had just left the castle that morning after filming for four nights straight. She finally found the keys and led us out towards the interior courtyard. It was a large, dark, outdoor area, only used as a walkway between towers. The stone walls were black from centuries of built up mold, reminding us how ancient the castle really is. In front of us was a large, stone spiraled staircase that led up to the very top of the tower. Built ages ago, the stone staircase was made for tiny feet. There were fifty, pie-shaped stair steps swirling up to the fourth floor. The heel of my foot couldn't even make contact with the steps, so I was forced to balance myself on the balls of my feet. When we reached the top, we stood in front of a door forged of ancient metal. As I cautiously scanned the area, I noticed that this castle was constructed in a different style of architecture from the previous castles I had seen. There were four towers, one on each corner, all four stories high and connected by four long **galleries**, each of which was three stories high. Hazel opened the door to our tower apartment called the "Lookout." As promised, we were to stay in the oldest tower that dates back to 900AD. The doorway was so low that Shante had to duck.

I asked Hazel if we could be shown the rest of the castle after we were settled. She coldly instructed us that we would have a tour the following night and the castle rooms were strictly off limits. Under no circumstances could we view the rooms until then. She continued with commands for us. The castle was heavily alarmed and, if at anytime guests are found in the other areas, they will be escorted off the property. At dark, the castle is locked. Guests may not leave and all cars must be parked on the side of the castle and out of sight.

She then gave us a quick tour of our apartment. Shante termed the décor, "Shabby Chic." As for me, I say leftover, well worn, mismatched furnishings are not really a style at all. Our apartment included a small kitchenette, a bathroom with a skull mounted on the wall, a living room with heavy velvet curtains and a master bedroom with a fireplace, a wardrobe, and dressing table. A smaller bedroom contained two twin beds and another cubbyhole of a bedroom that you had to climb a short, whitewashed staircase to reach. Above the cubby room's bed was a wooden trap door that led to the rooftop. There was a sign posted... "Do not enter! Any guest found on the rooftop will be asked to leave." Still, we found the roof a bit tempting as the door was unlocked and open. We could just see the night sky but, in the end, it was the ten thousand flying insects that proved the strong argument against it. Despite its well-worn decoration, the lookout tower really is an amazing apartment; it will sleep five, but is perfect for three. The tall windows in the living room swung open to an Italianate garden, with hedges trimmed to form elaborate designs. This night, the gusty winds swept through the apartment with a roar. The air smelled sweet and the ambiance of the entire castle left one to wonder what else, besides the usual ghost or two, lurked around these castle walls. The bells chimed at six and we realized we were now, definitely, locked in for the night.

As you can imagine, I couldn't relax that first evening as we sat in the apartment, sipping on **mead** and taking in the atmosphere. I got the sense that, despite it's deserted appearance, Chillingham castle was far from abandoned. It felt as if someone or something was watching us. A heavy, African stone statue held the window open with its pudgy body as the wind continued to whip through the thick red drapery in a wild fury.

Darkness fell, so we huddled closer together wondering what the night would have in store. We didn't have to wait long. Around 8 pm, as we sat down to dinner, we heard a faint growl inside the room. The three of us hushed each other and strained to try and hear it again as the seconds dragged by. Then, a much louder growl made Shante jump. It sounded like it came from under the table. Looking around us, I instinctively pulled my feet up before realizing that the growling was disembodied. No one dared move, Maliena's glass shook slightly in her frozen hand and the very air seemed stuck in my throat. But what could we do? Trapped eighty feet up in a small tower, there was nowhere to go. So, we did the only thing we could. We waited and, when nothing happened, we tried to laugh it off and finished our meal in edgy silence.

Shante located some guest journals that are kept in each apartment. She began reading excerpts out loud. "What's up with all the bats Sir Humphries?"... "Couldn't sleep last night, something was banging on the wall"... "caretaker told us the room next door was unoccupied"... "this place is scary, keep hearing strange noises." The entries went on and on; no wonder this place has the reputation as the most haunted castle in England.

Around eleven that night, Maliena was staring out the kitchen window when she saw twinkling lights in the castle's front, wooded area. They were very bright and low to the ground so we assumed it must be flashlights from other guests taking a late night walk or a ghost tour. I didn't remember until later that, when the staff leaves at 5pm, they lock the guests inside the castle. They also lock the castle's surrounding grounds to prevent trespassers and to keep guests from wandering around outside. A caretaker does stay in the castle in case of an emergency as there are no phones. And forget about using a cell phone... no service. Still, I kept thinking there was some way to leave the castle walls should you choose to. We found out the next night there really is no way out!

Around midnight we took a short walk down the spiral, stone staircase and across the enclosed courtyard to a museum type room. This is the only room open to guests. Here we found various pictures, including a painting of an older woman. She looks Romanian, gypsy-like, and her eyes follow you as you move about the room. There is an enormous, copper cooking pot from the 1200's that was large enough to hold twenty chickens and twenty pheasants all at the same time. In the back of the room is a small uneven hallway that cuts into the castle wall and leads to a holding cell. Here is contained a rather disturbing artifact in itself. When you enter the cell, which is not much larger than a closet, you see a massive, steel grate covered hole in the ground that drops about 25 feet onto more dirt and rock. At the bottom of this pit, lying as it has for hundreds of years is a well-preserved human skeleton. I know it seems unlikely but, later on, the staff confirmed that it was a real skeleton they had unearthed and simply left in place. The truth is, Chillingham Castle is full of skeletons, both human and otherwise. From the top to the bottom of this castle, you will see bones of various animals; even a taxidermy horse head, wildcat rugs, and cattle skulls... it's very odd and, well, chilling!

The first night was filled with frightening noises. There was a bell that rang every hour, giving off a hollow, haunting sound, cold spots that seemed to pass through us, bumps inside our bedrooms, and footsteps when no one was there. Sleeping was not really easy considering the unearthly racket around us, and none so much as in my room. The first thing that disturbed me was the wardrobe. It continued to make noises from the inside but there was nothing in there. It was a free-standing wardrobe with no rat holes, or air pockets that could have been responsible for the disturbance. Then, I began to hear footsteps along the base of my bed and by the fireplace. I wanted to run to the girls' room, but, instead, I pulled the covers up around me and tried to shut my eyes that were glued to the ceiling. Very early that morning, maybe around 4 am, there was that same beastly growl, but by then I was exhausted and way too scared to investigate. I was hearing all sorts of noises but, what I was most dumfounded by, was the one softer, more definitely high-pitched noise I had continually heard since night had set in. Suddenly, I was horrifically aware that the noise I had been hearing was that of bats!

The next morning came abruptly and I think we were all thankful for that. None of us had slept much, but we were still able to prepare for the long day as we headed out to explore the grounds. We made our way down through the castle doors and walked around to the side where we located what were once the castle stables. This area is said to be quite haunted and I had been pulled to this area almost immediately. Unfortunately, because they lock us in at dusk, we were unable to get down there at night when the energy would have been higher. On the other side of the stables, the ground drops steeply into a large dell that was, at one time, ideal for protection when the castle was attacked. We were told that the echoes from the castle literally float up the dell and over the valley almost four miles away, where even simple conversations from the castle can be heard. This was another advantage for Chillingham, because any skirmish warned neighboring forts of danger and they could send down extra soldiers to help defend the castle.

Our second stop was just down the hill, less than half a mile from the castle walls. Saint Peter's parish is a small, ancient church and graveyard attached to Chillingham. Everything is made of rough-cut stones, some of which are so old that you can see deep uneven divots where the rudimentary chisels had marked gouges in the stone that were too deep to smooth out. Inside the church were unusual gated wooden pews with waist high doors that lined each side of the red-carpeted aisle. Hidden from our immediate view, to the right of the altar, was the most unbelievable tomb I'd ever seen. From top to bottom, it stood about eleven feet high. The base of the stone tomb was carved with steeples and angels. The detail, considering it was made in the twelfth century, was so precise and intricate it took my breath away. The top of the tomb was carved into a bed, complete with tasseled pillows, upon which rested two, life-sized carved figures of a Sir Ralph Grey and his wife Elizabeth. Each figure lay with their palms pressed together and hands brought up to their chins as if in prayer. Their carved clothing told a story in itself. He was dressed as a knight, with a closely cropped moustache and a bowl haircut just above his ears. She was dressed in a long gown and a red cloak draped upon her shoulders, and her hair was worn up, shrouded in a tall, netted headdress. Every detail was carved from stone, right down to the row of tiny buttons on her sleeves. As a ray of light streamed through the windows directly onto the tomb, it was as if heaven were smiling down on them. This was the first and last peaceful moment I would experience at Chillingham.

After examining the Parish, I noticed that it was colder inside the chapel than outside. I told the girls that this is another church where there is a burial chamber underneath. After nosing around the outside, we saw a small grate that revealed the underneath crypt area of the church. We also felt a very cold draft that was wafting from the grate. Maliena walked down the stairs that led to a solid oak door which was shut tight and fitted with a padlock. All she could feel was the cold breeze that gushed from underneath the door.

As the day wore on we headed back and walked around the outside of the castle. We were looking around when a male grounds keeper on a small tractor stopped working and just sat there watching us. It seemed eyes were always watching us and it was very eerie. We headed for the formal garden which, when we looked onto from our apartment, showed very intricate designs. When you are walking through it, the hedges are six feet tall and it feels like a maze rather then a garden. Eventually, Maliena headed back upstairs to our quarters. After she left, Shante and I continued down to the end of the gardens and discovered a most disconcerting statue. At the very end, up on a small riser made of some mossy rocks and a tree, stood a white stone statue of what looked to be a Roman man. He was of medium build, neither too thin nor muscular. The statue was clothed in only a short toga across his hips. His chest was bare, his head was bald and his eyes were closed. The statue's hands were bound behind his back with carved stone rope. Bright green moss had begun to creep up the statue's body and was even attacking his left cheek adding a strange texture to the porcelain-like face. Perhaps even more troubling, was the fact that, on top of his head, a copper, barbed-wire crown, that appeared to be a replica of the crown of thorns, was nailed into his head with small rusty spikes. The soil that was mounded up to elevate the statue was soft and gooey, barely supporting the very unstable scaffolding around him which seemed to present more of a danger to the statue than had it not been there.

After all the excitement of the statue, we met upstairs for a light dinner and prepared for our three hour tour of the castle given to us by Arthur and another young man who worked security. It was a breezy night, not uncommon for north England, so I bundled up in a red wool wrap. We each grabbed a flashlight, and headed down the dark, spiral staircase to meet Arthur in the interior courtyard at 7:30pm. At the time we began, the night had fallen and it was pitch black outside. The stars sparkled above us in a vibrant display that we seldom are able to see, even in the country. The night was clear and cool and the moon was nowhere to be found. You could feel the intense energy of the spirit world merging together with ours, I have always found that there is much more activity at night.

Arthur walked us outside, about half way down the main drive, and beneath the heavy hanging branches of trees that so eerily hooded the drive. Telling us among other things that where the castle walls now enclose only a fancy Italianate garden, during the medieval times Chillingham was the only jousting court in all of northern England. He also said that over the many years of his guided tours he had been privileged by a regular visit from a wood owl. Arthur said the owl would often swoop down from the overhanging trees, flying past him and the guests, or let out a frightening screech, almost as if on cue.

Arthur stopped halfway down the drive and finally told us the first ghost story of the evening. Apparently, around 1925, a young woman by the name of Lenora was being taken by horse carriage to meet her new husband at Chillingham. The night was growing late and the pitch black of night had engulfed everything. The carriage driver, for whatever bizarre reason, would not drive her up to the castle. He stopped quickly and made her walk the half-mile up to the castle alone. She had only just started this journey when she became frightened and lost her sense of direction. Before hysteria could set in, though, a young man appeared and said he was the Lord Bennett's younger brother. He cheerfully escorted the relieved Lenora up the drive whereupon she saw her husband anxiously waiting for her. When she ran to him, she quickly turned back to thank the young man but to her shock he was nowhere to be found. Upon telling her husband about the man, he was speechless except to say that his younger brother had died two years prior. Obviously, his brother's spirit is very benevolent and is a gentleman even in death. I have said many times before that ghosts retain their same personality and intent as they had in life.

During the 1200's, this drive received the nickname, "Devils walk." Each time raiders were captured near by, they were brought to the castle where they would be imprisoned in the dungeon and tortured for information. If the captive became more cooperative, sometimes the jailer would tempt them with the idea of gaining their freedom. After they had divulged their secrets, he would lead them up out of the dark torture chamber, and tell them if they could run to the end of Devils Walk, then they would be free. Of course, a quarter of the way down, just when they thought they had a real chance, the guards would call up to the archers who would then shoot as many as fourteen arrows into them, starting with their shoulders, buttocks, arms and other non lethal places to insure maximum pain and suffering. They were used as human target practice. If the commander wanted to toy with the captive a bit longer, he would send the castle bloodhounds after them. Otherwise, an arrow through the heart would eventually end their suffering. Suffice to say, no prisoner ever escaped Chillingham castle alive!

After the Devils Walk, we were escorted off the drive. In front of the castle is a pathway through the thickets that the monks, as early as 900 AD, used to walk from the Parish to the castle. This trail is also the same walkway that leads from the castle to the coaching rooms; all three locations form a "Y" shape that was hard to see through all the trees, even with our flashlights.

Apparently, one of the coachmen was caught fooling around with a chambermaid in the nearby bushes, and as punishment; they hung him on a tree limb where he died. As you can tell, the history of this castle (like so many here in England) is not only haunted, but also horribly violent and gruesome.

This area is also where Maliena had seen the lights the night before. At this point, Arthur said that no one is allowed there at night for fear of a lawsuit, should anything happen. So, she told him about the lights we had seen the night before and he told her she must be mistaken as the the castle was solidly locked and there was no way for a guest to get out, or for any one outside to get in. Also, no tours had been conducted at that time. So the lights were not flashlights... but they were there, whether from humans or not... we know what we saw.

After our walk around the grounds, and taking one last look at the starry sky, the four of us returned to the iron clad front doors of the castle. The torches had been dramatically lit, creating an ominous scene, like what I would expect to see at Dracula's castle.

We walked through the oak doors, down the castle hall and through the steel-grated gate, where we saw even more torches hung on either side of the interior courtyard. One of the torches to the left of us continued to flicker on and off during Arthur's speech. He told us that it's a common occurrence and despite the fact that all the torches are new and full of fluid, they can never keep that particular one lit. Even on calm nights when there is no logical explanation as to why the torch shoots up fire and then goes out as suddenly as if someone blew out a lit match; the only explanation seems to be a supernatural one. We took several pictures as the torch continued to put on a violent display for us to watch, spraying up blue and orange fire and then extinguishing, only to flare back up minutes later. We also learned that the flying bat flag on top of the castle is Sir Humphries Wakefield's family crest, though it really does appear quite ominous above the castle, adding a menacing tone to the already stark setting of Northumberland.

During this conversation, I mentioned to Arthur that, since my arrival, I had continued to hear bats. He looked at me a bit stunned and said, "You're not supposed to be able to hear the bats. You must have exceptional hearing." Then, as if to give a reasonable explanation, he told me that the castle, among other things, is a bat sanctuary and there are four types of bats throughout the castle's grounds.

Keeping an open mind, it occurred to the three of us that, although there has never been any mention of vampire lore at this particular location, there was an uneasy feeling that this castle held more than just ghostly secrets. On the first night, Shante sat up later than Maliena and I. She really felt that something was watching her... something not a ghost and not human. All three of us were aware of this ominous force that seemed to be hidden inside the castle itself. The next night, as Maliena was coming up the spiral stairs for dinner, she glanced down at the window seal and saw a clove of garlic wedged between the panes of glass, like it had been placed there intentionally. There were also an absurd amount of mirrors throughout our apartment (three in the bathroom alone) and, if that wasn't enough to put vampires on our mind, the fact that there were stone crosses over each of the large glass windows. All the saltshakers were empty, yet the peppershakers were brimming full (salt is always used to protect or cleanse a home). This could be coincidence, but the parallels didn't stop there. It was as if something was trying to tell us we needed to take a closer look. Since our arrival, I couldn't shake the feeling that somehow vampires were associated with Chillingham. We all wondered why so many things seemed to point to either keeping vampires out... or in!

Finally, we made our way in to the first section of the castle. It was a large banquet hall fit for a king. Throughout this room, antiques and relics were strategically placed. Among them were a set of horse and elephant armor, along with a large Tudor table and red leather chairs bearing the Grey family crest emblem stamped on the backs. There was a sword over six feet in length, edged with real shark teeth from top to bottom, that dated back to the 1200's. Armor of all types were found in this room as well as African antiques and a stuffed bull's head. In a display case is a letter from the 1600's that had been found hidden inside the fireplace wall. The letter was written in old English and appears to be from a woman in the family seeking financial help anyway she could get it. This is also the room where Arthur told us about an interesting ghost story.

A little girl about five years old was accompanied on a similar tour with her father. Upon entering this room, she insisted to her father that she could see a Scottish piper sitting on an antique chair in the corner. The father did not see the piper so he shrugged it off as her imagination and continued to look around. But the child was persistent and continued to tell her father that the Scottish piper was now waving and winking at her. Her father finally began to think it was odd that his daughter would say such a thing, but the tour continued out of the hall and they left the piper behind. The next night a woman came for the tour and, when she entered the room, she was drawn repeatedly to the same antique chair. She stood by it several times and would put her arm on the back of it. As they left the room the woman asked the guide about the chair and the guide said, "Aah, yes that chair is 250 years old." He continued on, telling the woman about the child who had claimed to see the ghost of a Scottish piper sitting in the chair just the day before. The woman was thunderstruck and informed the guide that her father had died four years ago yesterday, and that he was a Scottish piper. She also said that she was supposed to take the tour the day before, but was unexpectedly delayed.

From here Arthur took us down into several other rooms, one of them a tower room made up as it would have originally appeared when the lords stayed there to keep safe during a siege. In this particular tower room, there was a trap door that had been covered with wood paneling, though a careful eye could still notice it. When stepped on, it made a hollow noise.

Maliena asked Arthur about it, but he was reluctant to elaborate. As we started to leave, two medium-sized bats flew down at us from one of the dilapidated staircases. The first bat was shy and stayed in the stair well, but the second one flew right past my shoulder and continued to navigate around us until we left. We now headed down into the apartments below.

The first **gallery** we entered had been grandly renovated to Sir Humphrie's liking and it really was very beautiful. Silk drapery hung on the walls, and larger than life-sized paintings of people, such as Elizabeth Grey, were displayed. While we looked around, Arthur talked about the legendary Pink room, in which a ghost supposedly haunts a painting. Supposedly, Lenora Tankerville's children and their nurse were awakened by a ghost that stepped out of a family portrait. This ghost continued to appear from the painting and would follow the children around until, finally, the children were moved to another room. Not knowing about the incident, a friend came to stay at the castle. The first night the family awoke, in hysterics, saying that a ghost had stepped out of a painting and was walking down the corridor. When the family located the painting, it was not the same haunted painting the children had claimed to see the ghost in. However, the painting was of the same female relative, now thought to be a ghost.

That is not the only ghost in the Pink Room. There is also the ghost of a small boy called the "radiant boy." When people stay in the Pink Room, they are often disturbed in their sleep by the crying and moaning of a small child. A ball of blue light begins to travel about the room, usually stopping at the foot of the bed and shimmering into a little boy before disappearing. During a renovation, ten feet of wall in the Pink Room was removed, revealing the bones of a child and some tattered blue clothing. Why the poor child's body was left to rot inside a wall is still a mystery, but the boy's skeleton was removed and laid to rest properly. The Pink Room was made famous by these two specters and is now strictly off limits to visitors. I did find it peculiar that we were not allowed to see it under any circumstances. In fact, no one ever is, with the exception of a few television tapings and, even then, only during the day when they can be closely monitored.

All of the rooms in this section of the castle were beautifully decorated. Between the two elaborate sitting rooms, there were several fancy Asian rugs, more cow skulls, animal rugs, and wall tapestries that dated back four hundred years or more. We were shown a broken, stone coat of arms that Sir Humphries had picked up from a gentleman only to discover, after it had been pieced back together, that it was originally from the castle. Many of the things Sir Humphrie's has bought for the castle have been discovered to originate from there anyway. Such was the case with a cloth tunic that Sir Humphries had purchased at an auction. Upon the tunic's arrival at the castle, Sir Humphries young son pulled on a loose string that subsequently unraveled a hidden fold inside the tunic, and exposed the Tankerville's family crest. It was then discovered that, centuries before, the tunic had belonged to one of the lords of Chillingham. As we began to leave the room that same bat made yet another entrance, it had apparently followed us from the tower above, teasing us with low dips past our heads.

The hallway through this area is home to yet another ghost. The "Grey Lady," said to be Mary Berkeley Grey, wanders about dressed in a Victorian dressing gown. Most often, the rustling of her dress can be heard as she crosses the cold stone floor. Legend has it that Mary's husband left her alone in the castle, with their infant, to chase another woman. Mary disappeared shortly after, but her ghost continues to wait for him.

One other ghost has been sighted in this area, although nothing is known of her other then the fact that she is wearing a white dressing gown and, if you see her, she will ask for a drink of water before vanishing.

The third room in this section was a dark, candle-lit dining hall. Arthur told us that Sir Humphries still likes to entertain special guests in this room. He had even made Arthur completely dismantle the electricity in the room so you can only use candlelight, as there are not even any windows.

The walls of this room were covered in what was described as Peruvian angel paintings. They were the oddest paintings I had ever seen. Each one was depicted as a different angel, but all of them showed what looked like Englishmen with long curly red wigs and weapons in hand. Flowing wings behind them framed their fierce pale faces. In the middle of these angel paintings is another painting of the only woman on this wall. It was none other than Mary Tudor, also known as "Bloody Mary." The painting depicts her as a very young woman and it seems to be deliberately placed in a central manner.

Mary Tudor earned the nickname "Bloody Mary" because she was a vicious ruler who burned hundreds of men, women, and children at the stake over religious conflict without conscience. She only survived as a ruler for a matter of days before Queen Elizabeth had her put to death. My question was, why choose to put a painting of such a horrid ruler up on your banquet hall in all her glory and surround her with warrior angels that appear to be protecting her? But then, who knows - there was also a rusty battleaxe mounted directly above her head tilted at an ominous angle.

Behind the Dining Hall is a large, open room with thousands of antiques piled up, giving the room a flea market feel. It was here that we made another particularly disturbing find. A small, Victorian baby carriage, that contained a babydoll-sized wooden coffin, lay concealed in a corner. I'm pretty sure they don't make toy coffins, so it must have been real. Unable to resist, Shante removed the lid from the tiny coffin and it revealed a ghastly sight. Inside the coffin was a baby doll wearing some sort of white, baptismal dress, but it's face was not that of a child. It had black searing eyes, a pig's nose, vampire fangs protruding from its mouth and a noose around its neck. After the initial shock, we tried to think logically about this. Traditionally, a pig face on a human body denotes Satanism, but it could also represent some sort of shape shifting. As for the fangs and the noose, we never came up with an explanation for that. We tried to ask about the doll and, like so many of our other questions, we were met with resistance. Arthur told us he did not know what it was, or where it came from... however he had extensive knowledge about the old, wooden, two-person toilet seat next to it.

Chillingham is said to contain ghosts from many time eras, including the Tudor, Elizabethan, and Victorian periods. Still, certain areas of the castle seem to have a much stronger connection to the spirit world than do others. The next room we were lead to, was the castle chapel which, during the 1920's, also served as Lenora Tankervilles private study. The chapel has a very high level of supernatural activity coursing through it, which creates a lot of restless energy. Lenora spent a great deal of time in here, and, despite the many people who claimed to see apparitions in or around the chapel, she was able to find her much needed solitude. One night while reading, an old piece of stone fell from the chapel wall. Closer examination of the hole led to the discovery of two skeletons. Like the fate of the Radiant Boy, the bodies of a man and a young child were found buried inside the chapel wall. Lenora had them removed immediately and their bones were consecrated to the ground. But there had to be some reason that these two souls were buried, perhaps even alive, inside not just any wall, but the chapel wall. Despite the questions, once the bodies were removed, Lenora insisted that their spirits were at rest and the chapel was at peace. Having said that, Chillingham castle has many ghost sightings to go with the many skeletons found over the years. Once a workman found the body of a man in a sealed room. The man was sitting in a chair and was so well-mummified that his skin was still intact. Unfortunately, when the outside air rushed in and touched him, the mummy disintegrated into dust.

Due to all the paranormal activity, Sir Humphries once decided to have the chapel exorcised, but, upon arrival, the priest said that the spirits were far too strong and they would have to wait at least seven years to try again. Seven years later, Sir Humphries called upon the priest again. He returned, only to say that the spirits of Chillingham were still far too strong for an **exorcism** and, more to the point, that they posed no serious threat. The priest said that the spirits wanted to stay so, after that, Sir Humphries changed his mind and let the spirits be.

After we finished photographing the chapel, Arthur led us down to a large kitchen keep that had the skull of a prehistoric elk. It's massive horns measured almost seven feet across. There was also a fireplace sunken into the back wall that used to have a spit large enough to roast an entire animal at one time. And would our night be complete without seeing three bundles of garlic strung together and hanging outside the door? We jokingly asked Arthur about it, but he shrugged and said nothing. As we exited the room, we were waiting in a small vestibule for Maliena to return with more film. Looking around, I noticed a large mirror on a door leading up to the spiraling tower. Taking a closer look, it dawned on Shante and I that this was no regular mirror, it was a two-way mirror; we asked about this as well, but we were again ignored.

The last bit of our tour took place in the torture chamber. This was supposedly one of four torture chambers throughout the castle. The other three are located in the bowels of the castle, but Arthur told us that they are still renovating, and it's not safe for people to go down there. The torture chamber is said to cling to the energy of hundreds of suffering men who met ill fates inside these walls. The ominous nature of this room again reminded me of it's violent past. I found it hard to believe that the room located directly behind the moat and in front of the courtyard, would be used to torture unfortunate prisoners. In fact, I would think that it was more likely used as a smithy shop, or maybe an armory.

Inside this torture room, there is definitely a lot of supernatural activity. One can just feel the vibration and instability of the air here. People have captured spirits on film in here, and we took several pictures as well. There is almost every sort of old, torturous tool on display with a hideous story to match. At one point, I felt sick to my stomach and refused to go in any further. It really bothered me to know that these objects that inflicted so much suffering are now used to entertain people. Most of the torture devices in this room were actually used back then which, I believe, is the real reason why there is so much supernatural activity in this room. There are nail-ridden barrels, used to roll small children down hills in, beheading blocks, rusted spears, quartering tables that pulled people apart. I also observed oil pots used to slowly boil prisoners in, a chair with nails sticking up from the seat, and even an old **iron maiden** that claimed the lives of more than 37 victims.

In this horror-filled room, the camera would not cooperate. It continuously focused in and out, even when Maliena was not touching it, and also took a picture on it's own. Finally, the tour was over and, by now, it was close to eleven o'clock. Despite the three hours it took to get through the open parts of the castle, I knew that this was only a small section meant to subdue the curious eye. Chillingham castle is vast, with almost as many rooms below ground as above it.

That night, same as the first, none of us really slept well, except maybe Shante. She slept in my room and Maliena slept alone in the other room. Shante and Maliena stayed up a while longer, and I excused myself to go to bed. As I lay in the darkness, I became aware of the noise again coming from the wardrobe, only this time it was more violent and aggressive and I became scared. I called out to the girls and, hearing my distress, Maliena entered my room. The wardrobe door was slightly ajar and, from a certain angle, we could see that the empty hangers were banging into each other even though there was no wind. Maliena finally took them down to make it stop. This made me feel better, but not much. Normally, it takes a lot to creep me out, but our entire experience at this castle had left me with an unfamiliar dread in my body, one I'm not used to. I found myself thinking that, if something were to happen to us, no one would ever know. My cell phone would not work in this area, so we had no ability to contact anyone. The last time our families had heard from us was at Dalston Hall. I couldn't even remember if I had mentioned our next destination.

The castle is isolated from everything even remotely modern. We could disappear and no one would ever know what happened, our safety was a concern.

Early in the morning, I got up to use the bathroom and saw that Maliena's door had been tightly shut. At first, I figured she wanted some privacy, but I still thought that was odd considering we were all so spooked and had intentionally left our doors open so we could hear each other. Assuming she had shut it, I left it that way. When I woke up in the morning, I asked Maliena about it and she looked surprised. "My door was open all night," she said. She had even woken up several times to use the bathroom and never noticed the door shut. It was yet another unexplainable incident at Chillingham. Finally, it was time to pack up and leave. I really wasn't sad to go; although Chillingham is a fascinating property, I never could shake that foreboding feeling that seemed to follow us during our stay.

We packed up the car and headed out the way we had come, down the long, tree-lined road. At the end, though, we found the gate padlocked with a heavy iron chain. It was very surprising to us that they had not yet unlocked the gate to allow guests to leave. After all, it was well past 11 am, and checkout had been at 10 am. Unable to find someone to let us out, we were forced to turn the car around and head back to the castle to ask them to unlock it for us. One of the women on staff walked out with Shante to give her instructions on which way to go. She pointed in the opposite direction we had come and said to follow that road down past the coaching house, the same way we came in. Shante responded to her that we hadn't come in that way, we had come in from down the Devil's Walk road. The woman scoffed at her as she walked away and said, "Sorry miss, but that's impossible. That old, gated road is always kept locked shut."

CHANNELED INFORMATION

Of all the stories I have heard about this castle, the biggest impression I got was the fact that some sort of mystical creature resides here. I am inclined to say that at one time this castle housed vampires, which would explain the unbelievable amount of skeletons found scattered around. Even in the most cruel of castles, it would not make sense that they would just leave bodies to rot throughout the castle or, even more bizarre, bury them within the walls. The human crypt keepers were servants that were mesmerized by the supernatural spell cast upon them. The humans would pass their job down from generation to generation to their heirs. They would themselves have protection from the vampire in return for their services. Today the people that work at the castle, are ancestors of the crypt keepers. They are still diligent at keeping the secrets of Chillingham from the outside world, and abhor curious tourists.

The Radiant Boy was a ghost at this castle but he has since then moved on and no longer haunts Chillingham, although a residual imprint of him can still be felt. He was buried alive in the wall and as my guides showed him to me, he was screaming when they walled him up which is why people hear him scream still. The group of men responsible for his death were apparently punishing him for his mischievous behavior. Originally, they had intended to release him, but the trauma put the child in shock which caused his death. Since the men had no regard for human life, and they figured he was dead, they forgot about it and left his body there.

My guides told me that the ghost in the painting was a made up story and that she never actually existed.

The man and child who were found together inside the chapel wall were attempting to hide during a siege. I am not clear as to the actual cause of death, but there are layers upon layers of hidden passages and tunnels and they were left there to rot and decay because no one cared enough to bury them properly. The excessive lack of concern, and gruesome torture games that the inhabitants of Chillingham partook in, were commonplace.

The growling was a dark entity trying to scare us. If you don't remember what a dark entity is from my previous book, it is a malevolent, non-human spirit from a lower astral plane.

The apparition who begs for water is an actual ghost. She died of starvation and dehydration, after being locked up somewhere in the castle, and was slowly poisoned, causing her with a continual thirst. The woman didn't understand why she was being tortured and still thinks she is in agony, which is why she begs for water, even as a ghost. This particular spirit roams the castle as well as the grounds around it, usually appearing in a simple dress or sleeping gown, and lived during the Victorian era in, I would say, the late 1800's.

I had hoped to channel more information about the ghosts of Chillingham, but my guides had other things on their mind. The most information I attained was about vampires. This castle was used to house them and certain humans protected their secrets as they continued with this arrangement for many centuries.

Chillingham Castle boasts the reputation of being the most haunted castle in Great Britain. It is most defiantly the most ominous.

*"The evil of the world is made
possible by nothing,
but the sanction you give it."*

- Ayn Rand

THE BLACK SWAN INN
DEVIZES, WILTSHIRE, ENGLAND

HISTORY

The Black Swan pub began as a coaching inn in the small town of Devizes. It dates back to around 1737, although locals say the building itself may have been built around the time of the town's original settlement, which dates back to 1088. The Black Swan is located in the heart of town, less than a block from the market cross so, no doubt, the inn has sheltered a vast amount of travelers throughout the centuries.

But the sleepy town of Devizes, which means "on the boundary", was not always so peaceful. Henry I raised a boy, by the name of Stephan, who was a direct descendant of William the conqueror. During the 1100's, he was forced to battle Stephan after refusing to give him the crown. As a result, a massive civil war erupted and Devizes was caught in the middle of it. Finally, in 1141, the war ceased and, for a time, Devizes and its people were left in peace.

The Black Swan has a very hard to trace and hushed history surrounding it. First of all, no one really knows exactly how or when the coaching inn took the name "Black Swan," especially since black swans originated in Australia and were not introduced to other parts of the world until more recent centuries. This fact leaves one to believe the coaching inn probably acquired the name later on. I did hear that it was originally called "the King's Crown" but there is no way to confirm this for sure.

There are also rumors that the Black Swan was a meeting place for such secret societies as the "Freemasons", not to mention that, under the town of Devizes, are endless tunnels that connect buildings together. They were used to exchange goods, cellar to cellar, and to smuggle things in and out of the town. There are a few stories that also suggest that underground brothels were attached to these underground passages as well. One thing we can be certain of is in the cellar of the Black Swan, there are at least three passageways leading out of the inn, but they are presently sealed up with brick and mortar. I've tried to find some more substantial information, but because there was a fire in the inn, most of the historic documents were destroyed. Also, much of the information that is still available contradicts itself. Hopefully, more of the history will be revealed during my channeling session.

JOURNAL
March 17th - 18th

We drove from Northumberland, down through the midlands of Manchester, and ended in the county of Wiltshire. This 200 mile drive, that would have taken us under three hours in the states, took us ten hours here in England. But we did make one stop in the small town of Lancaster to see the famous Lancaster Castle, home to what were some very famous witch trials.

By the time we parked and made our way up the steep hill to the top of the castle, I was already out of breath. No wonder this castle was never stormed... once you reach the top, you're too tired to do much else! Honestly, it was almost a 45-degree angle straight up a cobblestone road. Once we reached the top, we walked up to the enormous iron doors that were bolted shut. It seemed rather odd to lock a museum during business hours, but we weren't going to turn back now, so we did the most logical thing we could think of... we knocked. In retrospect, perhaps it wasn't such a brilliant plan. Try, if you will, to picture three American women, coats and cameras in hand, being greeted at the castle doors by a stern prison guard who wanted to know what the hell we were doing. Realizing this wasn't the museum guide we had expected, we looked around and suddenly noticed the large silver plaque that read "Lancaster prison" in bold black script. This might have been funny if the guard was not so perturbed. It turns out the English don't always share our American humor about such discrepancies. She pointed us in the right direction (which, incidentally, is in the back of the castle... go figure) and we made it just in time for our grand witch tour. And by grand witch tour, I mean grand "jury" tour! Our tour guide was passionate about his judicial knowledge and escorted us through the various rooms in the castle, speaking excitedly. He wore jet black hair to his waist, silver knuckle rings and black spider boots that fit surprisingly well with his suit and tie. Unfortunately, he had little information about witches. We were given a short story about the Pendle witch trials and unwanted information about the English court system. However, this Gothic tour guide did give us one important piece of information regarding the witch trials. He told us that witches in England were never burned, they were hung. This information, coupled with the fact that I briefly discussed witches in the first chapter of this book, was enough encouragement for me to begin researching the Pendle witch trials and it turned out to be a fascinating story.

The Pendle witch trials occurred during the reign of James VI who was a strong believer in the evils of witchcraft. As king, he used his power to see hundreds of people tried and hung as witches.

The Pendle witch trials took almost six months and involved three families that were tied together over a disagreement which had created bad blood between them. Apparently, a woman named Alizon Device cursed a peddler who would not sell her pins. Moments later he died of a heart attack. Alizon voluntarily confesses to bewitching him because of her guilt and proceeded to tell the magistrates that her grandmother (the widow Demdike) had taught her the art of witchcraft and had killed several people in their village. The widow Demdike confessed to this and also said that the Chattox family, as well as others, were involved.

The widow Chattox, the widow Demdike, Ann Redfern, and Alizon were all sent to Lancaster Castle to await trial. In the meantime, a witch frenzy had ensued and more and more fingers were being pointed. The main witness was nine-year old Jennet Device, who implicated over 15 people that she said were witches. Everyone they could find were rounded up and imprisoned, and although the investigation took half a year, the trial lasted less than a week. The defendants were denied the right to call witnesses on their behalf and, despite discrepancies from the prosecution, ten of the accused were found guilty and condemned to hang.

Jennet Device's testimony held the most weight with the judge. Because of her testimony, ten people, including her brother, sister, mother, and grandmother (who had already died in jail) were found guilty and sentenced to death. Immediately after the trial, all ten of the convicted, ranging in age from 8 to 80 were hung. Jennet Device was praised for betraying her family, but years later she was ironically accused of witchcraft herself and sent to jail, before finally being acquitted of the charges.

I think this case is perhaps the best in English history to describe the hysteria and false accusations that ran rampant throughout the villages. Gossip and backstabbing would set suspicion on entire families, accusations would fly and many innocent people suffered as a result.

It was very late at night before we arrived in the very small country village of Devizes. We were all aggravated by the day's drive and exhausted. The Black Swan looked probably much as it had hundreds of years ago. The Black Swan was built in the 1700's, but the building itself goes back to the 1500's. At any rate, the bar inside was small and cozy and we loved the casual feel. After settling into our uneven rooms, (because the floors literally tilted in a downward sway) we went back downstairs to join the pub's manager, Ben. After a few drinks and some great conversation, we began to look around the hotel. It was a dark night, and the hotel was very quiet. We were the only people still roaming about. Over the years, many people have died at the Black Swan and the ghosts still linger to prove it. The problem is, so little is known about the pubs history that it is hard to pinpoint who these ghosts were in life. Shortly after our arrival, we were told that only two well-documented ghosts are still seen today. The more reported of the two is a gentleman who appears to like the front of the pub. He is occasionally seen sitting in a chair, looking out onto the streets while smoking a cigar.

Right away, I picked up on a presence, not of a man, but of a woman at the front table in the bar area. Ben told us that the ghost story is of a male, so he had always recognized the presence as such. I assured him it was a female ghost; I felt she had worked at the

Black Swan long ago, as a prostitute.

After I spent some time observing this first ghost, whom no one else seemed aware of, Ben escorted us down into the cellar. It was a creepy area of the pub. There were four stone rooms that all came together, and one could see that, at one time, there were several tunnels (now sealed) leading out in different directions. I did not pick up on any spirits in the cellar, even though it is said to be the most haunted section of the pub. But, I could feel a residual energy in the cellar that is linked to the past. This area was once filled with different passageways into the city; people would smuggle goods to and fro, and it was also used as a brothel. Ben told us that the most recognized ghost in the cellar is that of a woman holding a baby. Everyone who sees or feels her, says that there is a feeling of panic in her. She seems to have an urgent desire to leave, but cannot. Again, I did not feel her, but I knew right away that the Black Swan had a scary and seedy history.

The last place that Ben took us was onto the second floor of a room called the function room. It was an oblong meeting room with a long table and, to the far left, was a bar set up to serve. Every inch of the room was done in beautiful, deep rich wood, ceiling to floor. One of the waitresses had a recent scare when she heard footsteps on the wood floor behind her. Maliena spoke with her about it the next morning. The waitress said she had been setting up the room for a meeting when she began to feel uneasy. She heard solid footsteps, but when she spun around to look, there was no one there.

I stood in the function room for a long while. No one spoke and only our breathing could be heard. The room had a chilled feel to it and I rubbed my hands together involuntarily. That was when I saw my first physical apparition of the trip. On the ceiling, right where I was looking, a perfect black orb formed no more than two feet from me. It was coming out of the ceiling in an oozing fashion. It swooped down about three feet and then glided up and over to the right side and vanished back into the ceiling. Maliena let out a gasp and pointed to the spot saying, "Did you guys see that?" Of course, Shante hadn't, but I definitely had. Minutes later I saw a similar orb further down the room, only this one was white, but it did the same thing that the black one had. We were amazed to see them and, as I glanced over to Maliena, her eye contact confirmed to me that, she too, had seen the second one. We walked further down the room and I saw yet another apparition. This one was in the form of a black shadow which moved across the far wall maybe four steps and then, it too disappeared. I believe it was the same ghost responsible for the footsteps the waitress had heard. To see three apparitions in one hour is really amazing. We stayed up a while longer, but the energy seemed to return to normal so we finally left the function room. The second well-documented ghost is a young woman who is always dressed in white. She is often spotted sitting in one of the hotel rooms, despondent and unaware of any living presence; when approached, she simply vanishes. It was now 2 am and we decided to call it a night.

The following day, the owner of the pub, Colin, was kind enough to take us into his office so we could see some footage that had been captured on video in the cellar. In the video, you can see several different floating orbs that continually whiz by the camera. They were not slow, as dust particles may appear, but moved very fast in intricate patterns as well as straight lines. For twenty minutes, we couldn't take our eyes off of the images.

Unfortunately, we did not see any other ghosts or paranormal activity during our stay, but I had all the proof I needed that the Black Swan was haunted. The problem I was finding here in the UK, was that the ghosts do not appear as regularly as they did on our

American tour. Hauntings are sporadic and, as time goes on, their energy fades away. It's inevitable, but that wasn't much consolation for someone like me who is used to seeing bizarre supernatural events constantly. The Black Swan is a great pub if you like a rustic old world atmosphere. Ben was very good to indulge us in our ghost walk, and the staff was quite pleasant. If you ever pass through Devries in Wiltshire, I would recommend the Black Swan, even if it were only to drink a pint or two.

CHANNELED INFORMATION

Witch Trials
"The Pendle witch trials"

My guides were very direct with this information, as I mentioned after the story, the ten people accused of witchcraft, were falsely accused. The king's magistrates were paid according to how many convictions they attained, so many of the accused that would try to plead innocent were simply tortured. Jennet testified against her family because she was pressured and threatened by the magistrates until she agreed. Remember, Jennet was only a child and easily frightened, so it didn't take much to get a testimony from her.

The Black Swan

The cellar is filled with spirits, which come in and out and use the cellar as a passageway, just as they did in life. The cellar is now like a portal, except that what was once a physical thoroughfare is now a supernatural one. That is why the paranormal researchers were able to capture so many orbs zipping around the room.

The Black Swan is a very haunted location, but don't expect too much activity at once. The prostitutes were not in the cellar, but men would come to the brothel through the passageways, the women would then cater to the men in the upstairs rooms.

The first night I saw a woman sitting in the front of the pub, she looked gray, and seemed to come from the Victorian era. Her apparition was faded and she was despondent, but she is the same ghost that has been spotted in the upstairs room and then vanishes when seen. In life, this girl was a prostitute who died from syphilis. She went crazy, couldn't eat and finally died. Because she didn't understand what was happening to her, and was very confused at the time of death, she remains as a ghost. Even today; her apparition appears ill looking and pasty.

The black orb, the footsteps, and the shadow of the man, are all from the same ghost. He was one of the previous owners of the Black Swan. He oversaw everything, paced a lot, and lived a stress filled life, as my guides showed him to me. He is also a more recent ghost, I say in the last hundred years; and only shows up as a shadowed silhouette or an orb.

"Men fear death
as children fear to go in the dark;
and as that natural fear in children
is increased by tales,
so is the other."

- Sir Francis Bacon

ANCIENT WILTSHIRE
ENGLAND

HISTORY

A ncient Wiltshire is filled with myth and lore. In the Southern part of England, about eighty-five miles west of London, the county of Wiltshire is home to mysterious **megaliths** and an abundant number of earthworks that were completed pre-written history.

Until this part of the trek, our plan had been to study specific haunted buildings. This was the foremost reason that we made plans to stay at the Red Lion, thinking that the stone circle that surrounds it would just be an added benefit. However, it soon became apparent that this segment of our journey would be more about the land than the reported haunting there. The tiny village of Avebury is steeped in history and the Red Lion has seen quite a lot of it, but it's nothing in comparison to the mysteries that lie at its fingertips.

Originally built in the 1700's, it wasn't until 1822 that the Red Lion became a licensed, public house and coaching stop for Avebury. The inn itself has a unique building structure, including interior walls assembled out of a white chalk paste and, like many of the older buildings in the English countryside, the exterior, white-washed walls have exposed, black wooden beams as well as a beautiful high pitched, thatched roof and red brick chimneys. Today, the Red Lion has remained in strong demand for the Avebury community, providing a meeting place for both locals and tourists alike.

Although, Stonehenge is perhaps the more popular of the two megaliths, currently a fence protects the complex; you can only view these stones from a distance. The Avebury stone circle is by far more impressive and still accessible. Built approximately in 3500 BC, it is also larger and much more intact with a circumference of nearly a mile. There are three circles inside Avebury and the smallest of them is still larger than Stonehenge.

No one knows for sure the true purpose of the stone circles; in fact, historians still debate as to who erected them. Many people theorize that the stone circle was built for the village's spiritual protection against the evil of witchcraft, werewolves and demons. Another popular theory is that it is some sort of astrological dial and that the two prominent stone shapes of pillars and diamonds represent the male and female aspects.

Regardless of the stone circle's original purpose, by medieval times the church had deemed it as a pagan worship temple. Soon after, there was a large siege on the circles and many of the beautiful stones were destroyed. Of course, they were so big that they had to be attacked very methodically, so some of the stones were buried, while others were bombarded with fire and water till they cracked apart. Destroying the circles did not come without a price; many men lost their lives during this process. In more recent years there has been an effort to restore part of the circle. Several stones were up righted and, under one such stone, an ancient skeleton that had been crushed centuries before was found. The stone had obviously fallen on him, instantly becoming his tomb.

Great Britain is also known for its twenty-four geoglyphs, which are huge pictures carved into the earth. Thirteen white horses have been carved into the hills in Wiltshire. One has been positively identified as prehistoric. Other similar Geoglyphs can be found in Egypt, Malta, America, Chile, Bolivia, and Peru. They are also mostly pictures of animals and the people that were indigenous to the area. As a rule, the glyphs are so large that they can only be appreciated and seen clearly if one is flying overhead. So we must ask ourselves - why would ancient peoples feel compelled to carve pictures that can only be seen from the sky?

While we were in Wiltshire, we realized that this is the site of many crop circles every year. Crop circles are created through the use of amazing sacred geometry. Globally, the formations have been reported since the 1700's. Of course, over the years, there have been forgers and fakes but the authentic crop circles that are intricately and mathematically detailed would be impossible to create overnight, by man. Like the geoglyphs, they can only really be appreciated from the sky. Scientists that have tested the affected crops have even found microwaves present and changes that take place in the plant cells.

Wiltshire is home to Silbury Hill, perhaps the most amazing of the earth structures as it is the largest man-made mound in Europe. Silbury Hill covers five acres of land. It stands one hundred thirty feet tall and the flattened top stretches one hundred feet across. This grassy mound has been carbon dated to 2500 BC. Local legend says it is the grave of a king and that he was buried sitting on his horse, but psychicly I know the mound is actually a giant, earthen pyramid.

Without a doubt, all of these earth structures had significant meaning to those who worked on them. Today, the puzzling architecture leaves us with more questions than answers, but we must give honor to the ancient peoples and their arduous planning and engineering.

JOURNAL

March 19th

Glastonbury and Avebury

We spent the first part of the day in a town just south of Bristol called Glastonbury, in the county of Somerset. This town was once an island where the famous legend of King Arthur and the Knights of the Round Table began. Arthur's body is rumored to be buried there at the Glastonbury Abbey, which is now a graceful ruin. The days of Arthur were a mystical time on earth. A period where majic was still alive but has since died.

We did see many artifacts and the famous thorn tree that took root from a staff that Joseph of Arimathaea had put into the ground. This is also said to be the site of the first Christian church which Joseph built in honor of his nephew Jesus. Glastonbury is a windy, steep-hilled village and very ancient looking. In the distance, you can also see a tall tower called the "Tor" way up on a hill. The Tor is believed to be a beacon on the isle and was lit like a lighthouse on foggy nights to act as a guide through the "Mists of Avalon."

Both Glastonbury Abby and the Tor are built upon Saint Michael's ley line (these are powerful energy points that naturally occur in the earth). In ancient times, many ley lines were marked here in England and important churches were built upon them. As I always tell groups when giving a lecture, "Mother Earth is a living being just like us." She has her own life force that are literally rivers of energy that pulse through her in which water, magnetism, and minerals all play important roles. Today, there are still some people that use dowsing as a method of water divining. Ancient man, though, was more in tune with the earth and was aware of the network of energy lines and their importance.

After Glastonbury, we headed to Avebury hoping to arrive before nightfall as the dark, single lane roads wind dangerously around turns, bends, and roundabouts. On this road, you are able to see the Silbury hill, which is Avebury's Neolithic mound. Silbury appears to be just a huge, grassy hill, but it's actually a very ancient step-type pyramid built from chalk.

We arrived in the village of Avebury just before dark and were amazed by the stone circle. Some of the rocks that surround the village weigh up to forty tons apiece. It's hard to believe that, before the days of cranes and heavy machinery to carry the load, the people of this village were somehow able to maneuver the rocks into place. They even used tools such as antler picks in order to shape the rocks to their liking. Over two hundred tons of earth had to be moved to create the Avebury Henge (the bank and ditch surrounding the stone monuments).

There are three stone circles that surround the village of Avebury; the large one on the outside, then two smaller circles sitting side by side on the interior. The two much smaller circles are older than the outer ring by about a hundred years being dated back as far as 4000 BC. Sadly, of the original outer circle that had once been comprised of 98 stones, only 27 of them remain standing. Of the two inner rings there is the Northern circle which was built with 27 stones, only four of which remain standing, and the southern circle that contained 29 original stones, and only five of those remain standing.

As we pulled into the Red Lion, Shante and Maliena walked out into the field on the side of the pub. There were two rocks next to each other and, when the girls stood next to them, they said they felt spellbound. Maliena told me she put her hands on the larger of the two rocks and felt a vibration running through it that she had never experienced before. To her, it felt as if the very breath of this rock was emanating through her. The girls wanted to stay near the stones longer because it had given them a safe and protected feeling, but the wind was picking up and it started to rain.

Avebury reminded us more of dangerous, mystical creatures roaming through the forest line than of ghosts and haunted buildings. The stones are thousands of years old and their purpose long ago had been one of spiritual protection from supernatural evils that one can't always explain away. Standing on the side of the road, looking up at the large swinging sign of the Red Lion, I was reminded of the movie "American Werewolf in London." Two American backpackers arrive in a small village in England and stop at the Slaughtered Lamb Pub on a blustery evening. As most of us who saw the movie remember, it was all downhill from there. That was exactly how we felt at Avebury, right down to the suspiciously watchful eyes of the locals as they drank from pints and whispered back and forth to one another. The ambiance of Red Lion was creepy at best and the three of us felt vulnerable inside the small crowded pub.

We walked into the bar which was filled to the brim with vagabonds who had gathered at the stone circle to catch the sunrise during the spring equinox on the twenty-first of March. There were a variety of strange people. Men dressed as wizards, druid priests in robes, hippie chicks in gypsy skirts, bikers and locals alike. Shante said it reminded her of a scene from "Mad Max." We continued through the pub and found a seat in the restaurant by the fireplace. After getting a bite to eat and chatting with our waitress, we were told that due to all the transients passing through Avebury, the Red Lion had chosen to confine it's bed and breakfast patrons to their rooms by 11:30 pm when the bar closes. To do this, they lock the hallway that leads down into the pub area. This was unnerving, as I don't like to be locked in anywhere, but they do this to prevent people from helping themselves to the open bar below. The doors were then unlocked the following morning at 9 am. Despite the emergency phone provided by the pub, we still felt very nervous.

With the abnormally large amount of people that overflowed from the pub to the picnic tables outside, I knew not to anticipate a great deal of paranormal activity at the Red Lion so I didn't spend a lot of time trying to investigate. We spoke to a few staff members and walked around the limited area, but there wasn't much to see. That doesn't mean that the Red Lion has not had any ghost tales throughout the years as they do have an interesting haunted history.

During the civil war, a cheating wife by the name of Florrie lived at the inn. Her husband, who had been away at war, arrived home unannounced only to discover his wife in bed with another man. Enraged with jealousy, her husband shot Florrie's lover and slit her throat, watching her drown in her own blood. After she died, her husband disposed of her body by dropping it into the inn's well. The ghost of Florrie has haunted the Red Lion ever since.

Florrie is not the only wayward spirit of Red Lion. There is also a ghost by the name of Beth which is usually seen wearing a blue dress. More often than not, though, only the sound of it can be heard as she invisibly moves across the bar. One of the most well-known sightings of Beth occurred when a custodian was picking up some glasses after closing. For a while, the Red Lion did not accommodate overnight guests, so the custodian had locked up for the night. Suddenly, from the corner of his eye, a woman crossed the main bar and left through the front door. The custodian thought at first that a customer had still been inside, but when he walked over to the door, it was still locked. The next ghost that has made the pub it's home is not well known, but there have been some documented sightings of the shadow of a man. Usually this apparition only lasts for a split second before vanishing.

It's not common for patrons or staff to see any of these ghostly images, but it does happen. However, the manager will tell you that it's very common to be plagued with missing items in his room, which he will later discover in a different location. Lights flickering on and off, and various objects levitating on their own, also occurs at the Red Lion with some regularity. Guests have also reported seeing dark shadows against the stark whiteness of the pub's walls, only to disappear when they fully turn to look.

As he was on his way to lock up for the evening, Maliena caught the night manager and spoke with him briefly about the ghosts of Red Lion. He told her that he had been working there for six months and had seen quite a few disturbances. A few times, he would go to sleep after setting his belongings on the night table, only to wake up and find them across the room on the dresser. He also said it was not uncommon for him to hear reports of loud noises made in empty rooms and other similar phenomena.

Although we could see the stone circle from the bedrooms, it was the worst night of sleep yet. It was hard to tell whether our lack of sleep was due to the energy radiating from the ley lines and the megaliths or from the small hard beds sitting on a very slanted wooden floor. Unfortunately, I did not have any luck in contacting the ghosts of Red Lion this part of the trip seemed to be more about Ancient Wiltshire's land and the earth's phenomena there.

We were happy to leave the following morning which was a drab, overcast day. An eerie fog settled around the people roaming about and the large, looming Avebury stones. As I stood by the car waiting for the girls so we could leave, I became entranced by a woman dancing in the rain with her three small children. She seemed oblivious to the passing cars and huddled groups of people in rain jackets staring at her, as she tossed her hands into the air and continued to spin around the children in quick sporadic circles. Laughing to myself, I thought, "Maybe she is the real ghost of the Red Lion." Shante and Maliena finally appeared and we quickly got in the car, leaving the dancing family in the rain and anticipating what London held in store for us.

CHANNELED INFORMATION

As I channeled information on the different places here in the UK it became more and more obvious that this book was insisting on a broader horizon than just that of ghosts. I felt nothing in the way of spirits while at the Red Lion, though I was told that Florrie is the resident ghost and still haunts the building. But most of the bumps in the night, and levitating objects, are a result of the energy that surges through Avebury, not from ghosts.

Stonehenge and Avebury circle
The Red Lion has disturbances with some regularity, in part, due to the fact that it is in the center of an energy field created by the stone circles. While many people think some ancient druid civilization is responsible for the construction of the stone circle, my guides told me they were not constructed by humans but rather star beings who used them like a portal for travel. It wasn't until much later that the druids discovered them and realized that they were magical. The stones were used for many different purposes, such as ritual ceremonies and spiritual protection, which is also why Avebury was built inside the circle of protection.

Ancient Geoglyphs

The Uffington White Horse that is made of chalk is not a horse; it is actually a geoglyph of a dragon made in ancient times. This glyph is more than 365 feet long and dates back to 1200 BC. The Uffington geoglyph serves the same purpose as other geoglyphs worldwide. They are a form of communication, a way of telling others a story of the land which is why each geoglyph portrays something unique to the area. Geoglyphs were also strategically placed where the energy could charge them. The Uffington horse, for example, sits on a ley line.

Crop Circles

If the truth be known, crop circles, geoglyphs, and the stone circles, all served the same purpose; they were built for communication. These structures were created by star beings but that information is meant for another book. The native Americans call these beings "The Star Nation." With the destruction of these sacred places and the shift in universal energy, Avebury is noted for its ancient earth works. But Crop Circles are still a regular occurrence in this area. If you get a chance to visit Wiltshire, England in the summer months, you could be one of those fortunate enough to see a crop circle first hand.

All of these sites in mystical Wiltshire will touch your soul, remind you that we are not the only creatures in the universe, and that the mysteries of Earth are far from all being discovered. As I always say, "It is presumptuous of us to look out into the night sky, see billions of stars, yet believe that we are the only intelligent life that God created."

*"Mystery creates wonder
and wonder is the basis
of man's desire to understand."*

- Neil Armstrong

THE LANGHAM HILTON
LONDON, ENGLAND

HISTORY

*L*ocated in the heart of London, the Langham Hilton was originally built in 1865. Constructed in splendor, the Langham held its superior title for years. Many famous people have spent time here, among them Princess Diana and several British film stars. There are over 400 rooms which provide its guests with top quality comfort and leisure. The hotel was completely renovated in 2000, and now includes a pool, gym, solarium, hair salon, and various other amenities.

Going back through time, there is a bittersweet story behind this legendary hotel that tells us not only of the buildings trials and tribulations, but of London's as well.

Unfortunately, the crash of 1929 affected all of London, including the Langham. Then, in 1931, the foundation of the hotel had to be reinforced because the new underground rail had inflicted damage to the building's structure. Finally, in 1934, the Langham Hilton succumbed to it's growing money related woes; it's stocks plummeted causing the hotel to fall into utter financial bleakness.

It took great effort to try and restore the hotel. In 1939, just as it looked like the hotel would make a comeback, Britain went to war against Germany. Managers went to war, guests stopped coming and room 24 was even turned into a first aid post. Once again, the Langham found itself without tourism, relying on local war efforts and the occasional English guest or two.

It didn't help that the hotel was being sporadically evacuated due to air raids. On Sept. 16th 1940, a bomb hit part of the Langham destroying the west side of the building. By the end of the war, two more bombs had struck the hotel, causing a devastating fire and extensive internal damage.

In 1945, the Langham Hilton was forced to close its doors. The BBC took some of the building space, and most of the hotel's insides were gutted and sold at auctions. The hotel was almost demolished but, at the last minute, it was saved by the Ladbroke group. Then, in 1991, after almost fifty years of closed doors, the Langham Hilton, having been renovated to its original Victorian décor, was once again opened for business.

JOURNAL
March 20th

The trip so far had been long, making the 85 mile drive from Avebury to London utterly intolerable. I couldn't wait for the comfort of an upscale hotel and plush taxi rides. Shortly after we left Avebury, the winds really picked up and it was raining heavily. Later that night, we would learn that several people had been killed in fatal car accidents resulting from the wind disturbance. The small car we were in was thrown around and the fitful weather was unrelenting but, thankfully, we arrived in London, unscathed, around 3 pm. After returning the rental car, we caught a taxi to the hotel and breathed a long sigh of relief.

The rooms here at the Langham are very nice. The décor was Victorian, but with a modern touch. The most haunted room of the Langham is room 333. It took less than twenty minutes for me to be certain that it was very, very haunted, but I'll get into that in a moment.

The ghosts of Langham total five altogether.

There is a Victorian man, often seen dressed in a black, full-length cloak as his ghost wanders the halls. He was said to have stayed at the hotel on his wedding night, only to murder his wife and then kill himself in their room.

The second ghost is that of a man who is dressed in military attire. There is even a well-documented record of him. Yet another victim of suicide, he jumped out of a fourth-story window and fell to his death. Since then, guests have seen him in various rooms of the hotel.

A coaching footman from the late 1800's haunts a room on the fourth floor, but he is seldom seen as he usually prefers to just bang around and leave cold spots for unsuspecting guests.

The basement of the Langham is home to some sort of an entity, though not much is known about it, and yet another entity has been felt on numerous occasions in the hotel lounge area.

The most well-documented ghost of Langham resides in room 333. This is the most haunted room in the hotel and there is a rumor that it contains, not only a ghost, but a **vortex** as well. The ghost in this room is also from the Victorian era and appears in the form of a glowing orb, sometimes shaping into a man. It's said that his entire body will take human form except for the legs. According to one reliable source, a series of heating pipes were added and, as a result, the floorboards had to be raised up. The ghost had already begun to haunt the room, so, in the spirit's reality, the floors should be two feet below where they are today.

We ate a light dinner brought to us from room service. The bigger of our two rooms was the suite on the fifth floor. It was lovely. There was a small sitting room and a large spacious bathroom made of swirling marble. At the end of the evening, Shante didn't feel well so she called it a night and went back up to her room for some rest.

Ghosts had been scarce so far, so Maliena agreed to stay up for a late night vigil with me in room 333. Before she arrived, I decided to take a quick shower. The minute I stepped into the tub, I got the sick feeling that a male presence was watching me. Then, halfway through my shower, a bar of unopened soap, which had been lying on the counter, flew across the room, seemingly of its own accord. I was hysterical. Frightened by this violent anomaly and, not knowing what else might fly at me, I cut my shower short, threw on a robe and called up to the other room to tell Maliena to please hurry.

Nothing happened for the next few hours and I almost began to relax. Later in the evening, as Maliena was preparing for bed, she opened the bathroom door, then stood, transfixed, trying to pull her eyes from the most bizarre spirit she had ever seen. It was of no particular shape or color, instead it was sort of chameleon like. The spirit looked like a clear bubble (the size of a beach ball), floating across the room and distorting what was behind it. We quickly shut the door, then, leaning up against it, she said, "We better keep the door closed. I don't think whatever is in the bathroom is too friendly." Remembering my earlier experience, I agreed.

We peeked into the bathroom once more, and the anomaly was no longer visible, so we climbed into the oversized bed and hunkered down for the evening. As soon as the lights were turned out, we began to hear and see all sorts of things. There was a screeching that persisted most of the night and seemed to be coming from the window seal. After almost an hour, we both heard a very loud banging noise in the bathroom, as if something had been thrown, but neither of us had the courage to go investigate.

I stared up at the ceiling and immediately noticed a black orb bouncing around. I really couldn't believe that I was seeing this, so I turned on the lights to find an explanation, but there was none and the orb continued to taunt us. I heard a loud crash to the left of the room and Maliena screamed. Something had pushed her camera off the nightstand. She wanted to leave, but I begged her to stay; after all this was why we were here. An instant later, I saw another large glowing orb with a distinct black outline rise up from the floorboards and float across the room. At the same time, several black shadows appeared along the wall and, again. I felt the strong presence of the male ghost. Like two small children, we clung to our pillows, debating whether or not we should make a run for the safety of our fifth floor room. After about a solid hour of this menacing activity, the noise died down and the orbs disappeared, but still we kept our eyes squeezed shut at the littlest bump. I was sure if I opened them, something would be staring back at us.

I knew for sure this was not just a ghost. It was either a poltergeist or a strong vortex. I spent the rest of the night staring at all the strange happenings and only dosed off for an hour or so. I think Maliena and I both prayed for morning and, when we saw the sun rise, we both started our day tired and haggard.

Months later, when we were putting this book together, we came across a story about a BBC newscaster who had also stayed in room 333. Giving us a shocking confirmation in his written article, he claimed to have seen a translucent ball floating through the bathroom door. He said that it was so clear that he could see the washbasin behind it, though somewhat distorted. He also said this ball felt very ominous! The newscaster's description of the clear orb was almost identical to the one Maliena had given me, though the sightings were nearly two years apart.

Room 333 is haunted. It has a horrible energy to it that makes it impossible to relax while inside. Although the hotel itself is in a great location, and remains very grand, just avoid that one room if you value your peace of mind.

CHANNELED INFORMATION

Unfortunately, I was unable to spend two nights at the Langham, so my only experience was during the first night in my room. It had proven more than enough, however. My guides were very clear in telling me that room 333 is a portal. It crosses over to a lower astral plane, which is why orbs are constantly appearing and disappearing. The portal was also responsible for the incessant, screeching noise. It's the same room that the male Victorian ghost resides in. This entity tends to knock things over and make bumping noises more than showing himself. When he does appear, he wears a cape and top hat and, in deed, his lower legs are missing. Room 333 has so many dynamics to it that it's hard to know where to start. The Victorian ghost is accompanied, not just by the portal, but also by a nasty poltergeist which is located in the bathroom. Not only is the clear orb part of the poltergeist, but the flying objects as well. In fact, the bathroom in 333 could prove to be quite dangerous for humans as this entity can do harm. In my professional opinion, this room should be sealed shut!

*   *   *

Thus ended my trip to the UK. I had to fight the urge to not be a little disappointed in the lack of supernatural experiences. I tend to forget that what is commonplace for me, is usually a once in a lifetime experience for others. The ghosts here in Great Britain are ancient; older than most of the ones in America by hundreds of years. They are quieter, and much of the supernatural energy is faded and sporadic. The castles and the land of Great Britain are historic and overwhelming; it is a place of mysticism and great adventures of old. For me to write about anything else would not have done this land justice so, in the end, I am grateful to Spirit and my guides for directing me toward these magnificent castles and pubs. I am reminded that each place on earth has a specific feel to it, usually one that cannot be anticipated, but most definitely can be appreciated. This is the story that I was meant to tell, so thank you for again stepping into the realm of the supernatural and traveling this road with me.

In Love and Light
Michelle Whitedove

The Langham Hilton

"When darkness is at its darkest, that is the beginning of all light."

- Lao-Tzu

8

RESOURCES

DALHOUSIE CASTLE
Hotel and Aqueous Spa
Bonnyrigg, Edinburgh, Scotland EH19 3JB
Telephone: +44 (0) 1875 820153
www.DalhousieCastle.co.uk

MELROSE ABBEY
www.melrose.bordernet.co.uk

DALSTON HALL
Carlisle, Cumbria, England, CA5 7JX
Telephone: +44 (0) 1228 710271
www.dalston-hall-hotel.co.uk

CHILLINGHAM CASTLE
Chillingham, Northumberland, England, NE66 5NJ
Telephone: +44 (0)1668 215 390
www.chillingham-castle.com

LANCASTER CASTLE
Lancashire, England
www.lancastercastle.com

THE BLACK SWAN HOTEL
Market Place, Devizes, Wiltshire, England SN10 1JQ
Telephone: 44(0) 1380 723259
www.theBlackSwanDevizes.co.uk

GHOST VIDEO SITE
www.visit.co.uk/mystical/index.html

RED LION INN
High Street, Avebury,
Marlborough, Wiltshire, England SN8 1RF
Telephone: 44 (0) 1672 539266
www.CropCircleConnector.com/Travelogue/redlion
99.html

AVEBURY CIRCLE
www.sacredsites.com/europe/england/avebury.html
http://witcombe.sbc.edu/earthmysteries/
EMAvebury.html

GLASTONBURY
www.glastonburyabbey.com

LANGHAM HILTON
22 Park Lane, Oxford Circus,
London, England W1K 4BE
Telephone: 44-20-76361000
www.hilton.co.uk

WHITE RABBIT LEISURE TOURS
Paranormal researcher Tony Walker
www.afallon.com/events.htm

GLOSSARY

aura - A persons electromagnetic field that radiates from the inside out. The part of the soul that can be seen.

caul membrane - An ancient name for the residual membrane from the amniotic sac that envelops the head of some newborn babies. (old English)

channel - A person who is used as a vessel for other worldly communication. Channeling information from the "other side."

clairvoyant - Clear seeing of psychic visions

close - A narrow alleyway that leads into a courtyard (old English)

crop circle - An authentic crop circle is sacred geometry. It is used as a method of communication.

cupola - A rounded vault, resting on a usually circular base and forming a roof or ceiling

exorcism - An exorcism is a ritual performed to remove spirits from a person or a place

gallery - A long narrow roofed area extending along the walls of a castle and supported by towers

ghost - A human soul that has remained earth bound

imprint - A holographic image that replays over and over again. A scene that has made a visual scar on time. Eventually all imprints will fade away.

iron maiden - A medieval torture device consisting of an iron frame in the form of a person in which the victim was enclosed and impaled on interior spikes.

jousting court - A long and narrow combat field, where two mounted knights compete against one another.

karma - A Universal Law. Science calls it: the law of cause and effect. The Christian Bible calls it: reaping what you sow.

laird - Lord, owner, master, owner of land estate (old English)

megalith - A very large stone used in various prehistoric architectures, notably in western Europe

mead - An ancient alcoholic beverage made from fermented honey

moat - A deep wide trench around a fortified castle that is usually filled with water

orb - An illuminated ball of energy which is a soul. This is the pure essence of what we are, our spirit form.

pele tower - A round tower stronghold without outer defensive walls. Common Castle architecture of border areas of Scotland

psychic - A person that can read an aura. One who can see events in the past, present, future.

scry - Scrying is an ancient method of foretelling the future. Using a black reflective surface such as pool of water, a smoked mirror or glass

spirit-medium - A psychic who also has the gift of spirit communication.

telekinesis - The movement of objects by scientifically inexplicable means.

telepathy - The ability to communicate information from one mind to another without using words. This is one form of extra-sensory perception.

wizard - One who practices magic; a sorcerer or magician.

werewolf - A person transformed into a wolf or capable of assuming the form of a wolf.

vampire - The undead. A reanimated corpse that is believed to rise from the grave at night to suck the life force from the living.

vortex - A transparent doorway made of swirling energy. A portal that leads to other realities.

*"I never wanted to go away,
and the hard part now
is the leaving you all.
I am not afraid,
but it seems as if I should be
homesick for you even in heaven."*

- Louisa Alcott

On Death

You would know the secret of death:

But how shall you find it unless
you seek it in the heart of life?

The owl whose night-bound eyes are blind unto
the day cannot unveil the mystery of light.

If you would indeed behold
the spirit of death,
open your heart wide unto the body of life.

For life and death are one,
even as the river and the sea are one.

- kahlil gibran

Excerpt of The Prophet

ABOUT THE AUTHOR

TV Talk Show host and author Michelle Whitedove is a world-class spirit medium. Since childhood she has communicated with the other side, relaying messages from guardian Angels, spirit guides and departed loved ones. Today with psychic insight, she uses her gifts to relay conversations from the spirit world to those open to hear the profound truth, conveying not only personal messages but more importantly, greater messages to illuminate the path towards self-growth. Her mission is to empower humanity, to bestow knowledge that we truly live forever.

Whitedove has been interviewed on ABC, CBS, FOX, PBS TV and NPR Radio to discuss the reality of psychic abilities and after death communication. With a full time schedule, she still manages to produce her TV show, lecture across America, teach spiritual development courses, and conduct private readings.

For more information and a list of appearances: **www.MichelleWhitedove.com**

Ghost Stalker II